Herbert John Webber

A second edition of Webber's

Herbert John Webber

A second edition of Webber's

ISBN/EAN: 9783337268565

Printed in Europe, USA, Canada, Australia, Japan

Cover: Foto ©Andreas Hilbeck / pixelio.de

More available books at **www.hansebooks.com**

Contributions from the Botanical Department of the
University of Nebraska.

NEW SERIES, III.

A SECOND EDITION OF

WEBBER'S "APPENDIX TO THE CATALOGUE

OF THE

FLORA OF NEBRASKA."

With a Supplementary List of Recently Reported
Species,

by CHARLES E. BESSEY, Ph. D.

(ISSUED JUNE 14, 1892.)

LINCOLN, NEBRASKA.
U. S. A.

PREFATORY NOTE.

The importance to Nebraska botanical students of the paper entitled an "Appendix to the Catalogue of the Flora of Nebraska," prepared by Mr. Herbert J. Webber, M. A., formerly assistant in botany in the University of Nebraska, now assistant in the Shaw School of Botany, St. Louis, warrants its republication by the University. It was published originally in the Transactions of the Academy of Science of St. Louis (Vol. VI., No. 1, March 12, 1892.) The present edition differs from the first only in the correction of a few minor errors, and the rearrangement of the index.

In his preface to the first edition Mr. Webber explains that "the names of those reporting species follow in every case the name of the species reported as it occurs in the Appendix. The collector whose name follows the species, it must be understood, is to be taken as authority for its occurrence, as in many cases I have not had the opportunity to examine the specimens. Thus specimens here reported must be understood to be preserved in the herbaria of those reporting the species, or in the Herbarium of the University of Nebraska."

The "Supplementary List" (p. 45 et seq.) includes all the species of plants added since Mr. Webber's paper went to press. It consists mainly of the additions made by Mr. P. A. Rydberg, a graduate student, in his collecting tour through the western counties in the summer of 1891, with others made by members of the University Botanical department, and Dr. H. Hapeman of Minden, and Rev. J. M. Bates of Valentine.

Specimens of nearly all the species reported in both lists, are deposited in the University Herbarium.

It is hoped that the periodical publication of accessions to the flora of the state will stimulate botanical students to a closer study of our native plants, and encourage them to deposit specimens of newly discovered species in the University Herbarium. To this end correspondence is solicited by the Department of Botany.

Address, DEPARTMENT OF BOTANY,
UNIVERSITY OF NEBRASKA,

MAY 25, 1892.
LINCOLN, NEBR.

CATALOGUE OF THE FLORA OF NEBRASKA.

By H. J. Webber.

CORRECTIONS.

(The reference given, is in every case to the "reprints" of the Catalogue.
g. = genus; s. = species; l. = line.)

Page 37, l. 36, for *foetidissima* read *foetidissima*.
" 38, l. 28, for *when* read *where*.
" 39, l. 13, for *at* read *as*.
" 41, l. 22, *Barns* read *Barnes*.
" 41, l. 29, omit *other*.
" 41, l. 41, omit *m ny*.
" 42, s. 5, for *flavo-fuscom* read *flavo-fuscum*.
" 44, s. 29, for *marino* read *marina*.
" 44, l. 6, for *diseasees* read *diseases*.
" 51, s. 165, l.9, *Aster ericoides* should be *Aster paniculatus*.
" 54, s. 204, "   "   "   "   "   "
" 62, s. 364. l. 1, for *salicini* read *salicina*.
" 67, s. 405, l. 32, for *cyndrical* read *cylindrical*.
" 69, s. 418, The host *Aster ericoides* should be *A. paniculatus*.
" 71, s. 437, l. 2, for *canadense* read *canadensis*.
" 71, s. 450, for *Œnothera* read *Œnothera*.
" 74, s. 477, for *Dittm.* read *Ditm*.
" 76, The remark under sterile forms should be — Suppused to be stages of *Ascomycetes* and *Basidiomycetes*.
" 82, g. 205, for *Pericularia* read *Piricularia*.
" 83, s. 640, for *Sporodesmium* read *Sporidesmium*.
  (As given by De Thuemen. Saccardo evidently unintentionally changes it to *Sporodesmium*.)
  Also line 5, *scirpiola* read *scirpicola*.
" 87, Order 56, for *Lycoperdiaceæ* read *Lycoperdaceæ*.
" 99. s. 952, for *aristulatus* read *aristatus*.
" 99, s. 956, for *schweinitizii* read *schweinitzii*.
" 122, s. 1342, for *lanceolatus* read *lanceolata*.
" 124, s. 1383, for *stolonifer* read *stolonifera*.
" 126, s. 1404, for *sinnate* read *sinuate*.
" 142, s. 1705, for *rush* read *bush*.
" 149, s. 1853, for *scrotina* read *serotina*.
" 149, s. 1867, for *eupatoriodes* read *eupatorioides*.

NOTES ON SPECIES BEFORE REPORTED.

(The number preceding each, is the species number in the main Catalogue.)

151. CYSTOPUS TRAGOPOGONIS (Pers.) Schroet. On Wild worm-wood (*Artemesia canadensis*), Pine Ridge, Aug., 6 (Webber).

414. GYMNOSPORANGIUM MACROPUS L. 'Stage II (*Ræstelia pirata Thaxter.*) On leaves of Crab Apple (*Pirus coronaria*) Butler Co., and Lincoln (Bessey).

416. PHRAGMIDIUM SPECIOSUM Fr. The specimens referred to Stage II of this species should be Stage I of *Phragmidium subcorticium* (Schrank) Wint. (See No. 81 of this paper).

520. ASCOCHYTA SMILACIS Ell & Ev. should be of Ell. & Mart. or following Saccardo the nomenclature should be changed to *Stegonospora smilacis* (Ell. & Mart.) Sacc.

622. RAMULARIA VIRGAUREÆ Thuem. On *Solidago canadensis* only, not on *S. rigida* and *S. memoralis*.

709. PODOSPORIUM RIGIDUM Schw. On grape stems only, not on *Physalis*.

886. WOODSIA OREGANA Eaton (Localities omitted in Cat.) Collected at Pine Ridge; Hat Creek Basin; Dismal River, Thomas Co. (Webber).

924. CAREX GRISEA Wahl. (Reported from Coulter's Manual). Ashland, May. (Williams).

926. CAREX JAMESII Torr. var. NEBRASKENSIS (Dew.) Bailey (Reported from Coulter's Manual). Hat Creek Basin, Sioux Co., Aug.; Broken Bow, July; Anselmo, July. (Webber).

929. CAREX LONGIROSTRIS Torr. (Reported from Gray's Manual). Dismal River, Thomas Co., July 12. (Webber). Ashland, Weeping Water, War Bonnet. (Williams).

1088. JUNCUS FILIFORMIS L. (Reported from Gray's Manual). Lawrence Fork Bottoms, Banner County (Rydberg).

1103. NOTHOSCORDUM STRIATUM (Jacq.) Kunth. (Reported from Coulter's Manual). Crete, rare (Swezey).

1126. QUERCUS NIGRA L. (Reported from Gray's Manual). Pawnee Co. (Bessey).

1187. ERIOGONUM ALATUM MICHX. (Reported from Coulter's Manual). Hills. Deuel Co. and Banner Co. (Rydberg).

1197. ATRIPLEX NUTTALLII Watson, is the prevailing *Atriplex* of N. W. Nebraska in the "Bad lands," etc., but is quite rare in the eastern part of the state where *A. patula* var *hastata* is the common form. (Webber).

1202. AMARANTUS CHLOROSTACHYS Willd. of Swezey's Nebr. Fl. Plants p. 13 is likely *Acnida tuberculata* Moq. (Webber).

1213. ARENARIA PUNGENS Nutt. must probably be considered as A. hookeri Nutt. See this appendix No. 269. (Webber.)

1257. NELUMBO LUTEA (Willd.) Pers. (Reported from Gray's Manual). Lakes, etc., plentiful. Fremont, July. (Williams & Bessey).

1302. ELATINE TRIANDRA Schkuhr (Reported from Coulter's Manual). Exeter, Sept. communicated by Dr. Wibbe (Bessey).

1398. MENTZELIA LEVICAULIS Torr. & Gr. should be changed to *Mentzelia nuda* (Pursh.) Torr. & Gr. It is the common Mentzelia of Nebraska. Mr. Rydberg adds the following note in regard to his specimens collected in Deuel and Banner counties: — "They agree in every respect with Torrey & Gray's description of *M. nuda* except that they have a bracteate calyx. In Porter and Coulter's Fl. Col. *M. nuda* is described as having a bracteate calyx." (Webber).

1491. ASTRAGALUS FLEXUOSUS Dougl. (Reported from Coulter's Manual). Lewellen, Common (Swezey).

1497. ASTRAGALUS MICROLOBUS Gray (Reported from Coulter's Manual). Cultivated ground. Deuel Co., June 25; Cheyenne Co., Aug. 13 (Rydberg).

1499. ASTRAGALUS MISSOURIENSIS Nutt. (Reported from Coulter's Manual). Curtis, Frontier Co., June 22; North of Kimball, Aug. 16 (Rydberg). War Bonnet Canon, June (Williams).

1501. ASTRAGALUS PECTINATUS Dougl. (Reported from Coulter's Manual). Prairies, near Gering July 20 and Pleasant Valley, Scotts Bluff Co., July 28 (Rydberg).

1504. ASTRAGALUS RACEMOSUS Pursh. (Reported from Coulter's Manual). Hills, Curtis, Frontier Co., June 22 (Rydberg).

1559. GILIA IBERIDIFOLIA Benth. (Reported from Coulter's Manual). Cliffs and Canons of Banner and Scott's Bluff Counties, July (Rydberg).

MERTENSIA LANCEOLATA (Pursh) DC. Swezey's Nebr. Fl. Plants, p. 11, should be *Pentstemon cæruleus* number 1612 of the catalogue.

1580. ECHINOSPERMUM REDOWSKII (Hornem.) Lehm. is the var. *occidentale* Watson. Since collected at Dismal River, Thomas Co., July 13; Pine Ridge, July 21 (Webber).

1581. ECHINOSPERMUM REDOWSKII (Hornem.) Lehm. var. CUPULATUM Gray (Reported from Coulter's Manual). Alliance, Aug. 6 (Webber). Chadron (Bates). Venango, Perkins Co., June 23 (Rydberg).

1589. PHYSALIS LANCEOLATA Michx. var. LEVIGATA Gray. (Reported from Coulter's Manual). Old fields, etc. Weeping Water, July (Williams).

PENTSTEMON GLABER Pursh var. UTAHENSIS Watson. Swezey's Nebr. Flowering Plants p. 12, should be *P. haydeni* Watson (see this appendix No. 364) (Webber).

611. PENTSTEMON ALBIDUS Nutt. (Reported from Gray's Manual). Antelope Co., Aug.; Anselmo, July; Thedford, July; Hat. Creek Basin, Aug. (Webber).

1666. GENTIANA CALYCOSA Griseb.   All of my Nebraska material of this species should be labeled *G. puberula* Michx.   (Webber).

1738. CNICUS PITCHERI Torr. should be *C. undulatus* (Nutt.)   Gray.   var. *canescens* (Nutt.)   Gray.   (See this appendix No. 391.)   (Webber).

1792. HELIANTHUS PETIOLARIS Nutt. var. CANESCENS Gray.   (Reported from Gray's Syn. Flora).   Lawrence Fork Bottoms, Banner county (Rydberg).

1804. FRANSERIA DISCOLOR Nutt.   (Reported from Coulter's Manual).   Prairies, Kearney County; Dix, Kimball Co., Aug. 14 (Rydberg).

ERIGERON GLABELLUS Nutt. of Swezey's Nebr. Fl. Pl. p. 9 should be *E. macranthus* Nutt. (See this appendix No. 411)

1836. ASTER TANACETIFOLIUS (Nees) H. B. K.   (Reported from Coulter's Manual).   Banner Co., etc.   Common in the western part of the State (Rydberg).

1867. KUHNIA EUPATORIOIDES L. var. CORYMBULOSA Torr. and Gr.   (Reported from Coulter's Manual).   Canous, Banner Co. (Rydberg).

The following tabulated list of new localities for Flowering Plants before reported was prepared by Mr. Rydberg from his collections. Some species are greatly extended in range, and some shown to be much more common than was supposed.

	BANNER CO.								DEUEL CO.				KEARNEY CO.							
Table Land	Hills	Cliffs and Sides of Canons	Canons	"Sand draws."	Lawrence Fork Bottoms	Pumpkin Seed Valley	Hackberry Springs	High Prairies	Hills	Cliffs and Sides of Canons	Canons	"Sand-draws."	Lady Pole Creek	Sand Hills	Prairies	Platte R. and Bottom	POLK CO.	LANCASTER CO.	SAUNDERS CO.	FREMONT AND FREMONT ISLAND
	898																			
																				900
																910		911	916	915
																			980	
																			1001	
					1008			1012												
1012	1025				1015	1082		1014												
1014					1089		1089													1081
	1105				1145		1114	1105												
	1169						1160													1147
1188							1188			1189										1166
																		1196		1184
																				1199
													1200							1252
	1209	1219	1252	1258		1207			1208	1258	1291		1201							1260
			1254	1288		1235				1288	1289									
										1289										
	1330	1322	1327	1348				1308	1322	1327	1348		1312	1320		1311	1352			
	1304	1361	1345					1394		1386	1353					1320				
	1395	1363	1355					1395		1388	1359									
		1369	1386					1397												
			1388																	
1408	1424		1416	1404			1434	1413	1401		1452	1402	1403		1413	1457	1413	1473		1423
1413	1482		1429	1453				1439				1404				1465	1482			1470
	1483		1452					1495				1453								1477
	1485																			
1578	1505	1507	1549		1537			1505	1513			1551			1511	1518	1541	1520	1522	1534
1580	1521				1556			1581				1556				1523	1595			1545
																				1599
	1643	1697	1664		1677	1601	1638	1609	1656	1685	1661	1676			1656	1668			1608	1668
					1682	1687	1641	1647												1610
						1693	1693	1648												1625
								1657												1626
																				1632
																				1637
																				1662
																				1686
1717	1752				1725	1755	1777	1737								1737		1717	1717	1720
1780	1756				1747			1739												1751
1797	1778							1772												1774
1798																				
	1848				1859	1809			1861			1859							1806	
	1849					1819														
	1861																			

PROTOPHYTA.

1. RETICULARIACEÆ.

1. RETICULARIA Bull.

    1. R. LYCOPERDON Bull. On decaying trunks of trees. Pine Ridge, Dawes Co., July (Webber).

2. CLATHROPTYCHIACEÆ.

2. ENTERIDIUM Ehr.

    2. E. ROZEANUM (Rost.) Wingate. (*Reticularia* [?] *rozeana* Rost.). Lincoln (Webber).

3. STEMONITACEÆ.

3. STEMONITIS Gled.

    3. S. WEBBERI Rex. (N. sp. in lit. Published in Pro. Acad. Nat. Sci. of Phila., 1891). On old stump, Lincoln, September (Webber).

4. PHYSARACEÆ.

4. PHYSARUM Pers.

    4. P. LIVIDUM Rost. (*Spumaria licheniformis* Schw.) On bark of tree, Lincoln (Webber).

    5. P. PETERSII B. and C. On bark of old Cottonwood and Boxelder trees, Weeping Water (Williams).

5. BACTERIACEÆ.

5. BACILLUS Cohn.

    6. B. SORGHI Burrill. On leaves and culms of Bushy blue stem (*Andropogon nutans*), Lincoln; Johnson grass (*Andropogon sorghum* var. *halepensis*), Howard Co.; and on numerous varieties of *Sorghum* grown on the Nebraska Experimental Farm at Lincoln. Quite destructive, forming large irregular purple patches (Webber).

6. NOSTOCACEÆ.

6. GLŒOTRICHIA Ag.

    7. G. NATANS Thur. Floating in stagnant water. Greenwood, July (Williams). Minden, attached to *Nitella* stems (Bessey).

7. LYNGBYA Ag. and Thur.

    8. L. CINCINNATA Kg. Minden. In material collected by Dr. Hapeman (Bessey).

8. CYLINDROSPERMUM Kg.

    9. C. COMATUM Wood. Minden (Hapeman).

ZYGOPHYTA.

7. PALMELLACEÆ.

9. TETRASPORA Ag.

10. T. EXPLANATA (Kg.) Kirch. Minden. In material collected by Dr. Hapeman (Bessey).

10. SORASTRUM Kg.

11. S. SPINULOSUM Kg. Minden. In material collected by Dr. Hapeman (Woods).

11. HYDRODICTYON Roth.

12. H. UTRICULATUM Roth. Stagnant water, plentiful. Fremont, July 31 (Williams). Lincoln (Bessey).

12. PEDIASTRUM Meyen.

13. P. ANGULOSUM (Ehrb.) Menegh. (*P. biradiatum* Meyen). In material collected by Dr. Hapeman at Minden. (Woods).

14. P. PERTUSUM Kg. var. CLATHRATUM A. Br. (*P. duplex* Meyen). Minden. In material collected by Dr. Hapeman (Woods).

8. PITHOPHORACEÆ.

13. PITHOPHORA Wittr.

15. P. AFFINIS Nordst. In stagnant or slow running water. Greenwood, July (Williams).

9. ULOTHRICHACEÆ.

14. STIGEOCLONIUM Kg.

16. S. FASTIGIATUM Kg. Minden. In material collected by Dr. Hapeman (Bessey).

15. APHANOCHÆTE A. Br.

17. A. GLOBOSA (Nord.) Wolle. form. MINOR Nordst. growing on *Nitella*, in material from Minden collected by Dr. Hapeman. (Woods).

10. DESMIDIACEÆ.

16. DESMIDIUM Ag.

18. D. SWARTZII Ag. Minden. In material collected by Dr. Hapeman (Bessey).

17. SPHÆROZOSMA Corda.

19. P. SERRATUM Bailey. Minden. In material collected by Dr. Hapeman (Bessey).

18. SPIROTÆNIA Breb.

20. S. CONDENSATA Breb. In material from Minden, collected by Dr. Hapeman.

19. COSMARIUM Corda.
    21. C. broomei Thwaitos. In material from Minden, collected by Dr. Hapeman Oct. 19 (Woods).

20. XANTHIDIUM Ehrb.
    22. X. fasciculatum (Ehrb.) Ralfs. In material from Minden, collected by Dr. Hapeman (Woods).

21. ARTHRODESMUS Ehrb.
    23. A. octocornis Ehrb. In material from Minden, collected by Dr. Hapeman (Woods).

22. EUASTRUM Ehrb.
    24. E. inerme Lund. In material from Minden, collected by Dr. Hapeman (Woods).

23. MICRASTERIAS Ag.
    25. M. americana (Ehrb.) Kg. Minden, in material collected by Dr. Hapeman (Woods).
    26. M. speciosa Wolle. Minden. In material collected by Dr. Hapeman (Woods).

24. STAURASTRUM Meyen.
    27. S. aristiferum Ralfs. Minden. In material collected by Dr. Hapeman (Woods).

11. DIATOMACEÆ.
25. GOMPHONEMA.
    28. G. acuminatum Ehrb. var. laticeps Ehrb. Minden. In material collected by Dr. Hapeman. (Bessey).

12. ENTOMOPHTHORACEÆ.
26. EMPUSA Cohn.
    29. E. aphidis Hoffman. On *Aphis* Sp. on *Polygonum*. Ashland. Oct. (Williams).

OOPHYTA.

13. ŒDOGONIACEÆ.
27. ŒDOGONIUM Lk.
    30. Œ. borisianum (Le Cl.) Wittr. In material from Minden collected by Dr. Hapeman (Woods).
    31. Œ. delicatum Kg. Minden. In material collected by Dr. Hapeman (Bessey).

28. BULBOCHÆTE Ag.
    32. B. polyandra. Cleve. Minden. In material collected by Dr. Hapeman (Bessey).

14. PERONOSPORACEÆ.

29. PERONOSPORA Corda.

33. P. OXYBAPHI Ell. & Kell On leaves and young shoots of *Oxybaphus nyctagineus*, causing much damage to the host. Elmwood, Ashland. June and July (Williams).

30. PLASMOPARA Schroet.

34. P. HALSTEDII (Farlow) Berl. and De Toni. On leaves of Sunflower (*Helianthus annuus*), Lincoln, Oct. (Webber). Great ragweed (*Ambrosia trifida*), Wabash, Aug. (Williams).

31. SCLEROSPORA Schroet.

35. S. GRAMINICOLA (Sacc.) Schroet. (*Peronospora graminicola* Sacc.) On Green and Yellow fox-tail (*Setaria viridis* and *S. glauca*), Ashland, Weeping Water (Williams). Lincoln (Bessey).

32. CYSTOPUS Lev.

36. C. IPOMOEÆ-PANDURANÆ (Sacc.) Farlow. On leaves and petioles of Morning Glory (*Ipomœa* Sp.) Richardson Co., Aug. (Webber); Ashland (Williams). Very destructive, variously twisting and distorting the leaves and petioles, finally causing them to drop off.

CARPOPHYTA.

15. COLEOCHAETACEÆ.

33. COLEOCHAETE Breb.

37. C. IRREGULARIS Pringsh. Minden. In material collected by Dr Hapeman (Bessey).

38. C. ORBICULARIS Pringsh. Minden. In material collected by Dr. Hapeman (Bessey).

16. ERYSIPHEÆ.

34. ERYSIPHE Hedw.

39. E. GRAMINIS DC. Conidia stage (*Oidium monilioides* Link.) On leaves of Wild Rye (*Elymus canadensis*), Weeping Water (Williams).

The Oidium is the only stage frequently found here. I have frequently observed this at Lincoln on various grasses, but have never found the perithecia (Webber).

17. SPHÆRIACEÆ.

35. CHÆTOMIUM Kunze.

40. C. CHARTARUM Ehrenb. On decaying broom. Lincoln (Pound).

36. PHYSALOSPORA Niessl.

41. P. MEGASTOMA (Peck) Sacc. On leaves of *Astragalus drummondii*. Belmont, Dawes Co., July. Quite destructive (Webber).

37. SPHÆRELLA Ces. & DeNot.

    42. S. OPUNTIÆ Ell. & Ev.   On Cactus (*Opuntia missouriensis*), Weeping Water (Williams).

18. HYPOCREACEÆ.

38. NECTRIELLA Sacc.

    43. N. VULPINA (Cke.) Berl. & Vogl.   On old decaying log, Lincoln (Webber).

19. DOTHIDIACEÆ.

39. PHYLLACHORA Nitschke.

    44. P. LESPEDEZÆ (Schw.) Sacc.   On Bush clover (*Lespedeza frutescens*), Nemaha Co., Oct. (Webber).

40. PLOWRIGHTIA Sacc.

    45. P. RIBESIA (Pers.) Sacc.   On stems of gooseberry (*Ribes gracile*), Ashland (Williams).

20. HYSTERIACEÆ.

41. HYSTEROGRAPHIUM Corda.

    46. H. FRAXINI (Pers.) DeNot   On Ash (*Fraxinus viridis*) Lincoln (Pound).

21. CALICIACEÆ.

42. ACOLIUM Ach.

    47. A. TIGILLARE Ach.   On Sandstone, rare.   Pine Ridge, Aug. (Webber).

22. GRAPHIDIACEÆ.

43. ARTHONIA (Ach.) Nyl.

    48. A. RADIATA (Pers.) Th. Fr.   On Hickory bark.   Milford, Oct. (Webber).

44. OPEGRAPHA (Humb.) Ach. Nyl.

    49. O. VARIA Pers. var. PULICARIS.   Bark of trees.   Weeping Water (Williams).

23. LECIDEACEÆ.

45. BUELLIA De Not., Tuckerm.

    50. B. EPIGÆA (Pers.) Tuckerm.   On high sandy ground.   Pine Ridge, Aug. (Webber).

46. LECIDEA (Ach., Fr.) Tuckerm.

    51. L. TESSELLATA Floerk.   On stone.   Pine Ridge, Aug. Common. (Webber).

47. BIATORA, Fr.

    52. B. MUSCORUM (Sw.) Tuckerm.   On moss.   Pine Ridge, Aug. (Webber).

53. B. RUSSULA (Ach.) Mont. f. DEALBATA Tuckerm. On earth etc.
Valentine, Harrison (Williams).

48. CLADONIA Hoffm.
    54. C. BOTRYTIS (Hag.) Hoffm. Rotten Pine log. War Bonnet canon,
    N. W. Nebraska. (Williams).
    55. C. CARIOSA (Ach.) Spreng. On ground under trees on bluffs and
    in damp places, very common. Pine Ridge, Aug.; Dismal River,
    Thomas Co., July (Webber); War Bonnet canon (Williams).

24. PARMELIACEÆ.

49. URCEOLARIA Ach.
    56. U. SCRUPOSA (L.) Nyl. On sandy ground and sandstone, common.
    Pine Ridge, July (Webber).

50. LECANORA Ach. Tuckerm.
    57. L. BRUNONIS Tuckerm. On sandstone, Ashland. (Williams).
    58. L. GLAUCOCARPA (Wahl.) Ach. On stone, common. Pine Ridge,
    Aug. (Webber).
    59. L. PRIVIGNA (Ach.) Nyl. On stone. Pine Ridge, Aug. (Webber).
    60. L. SCHLEICHERI (Ach.) Nyl. On ground, abundant. Pine Ridge,
    Aug. (Webber).
    61. L. VARIA (Ehrh.) Nyl. var. S.EPINCOLA Fr. On bark of pine, com-
    mon. Pine Ridge, Aug. (Webber). On trees, Ashland. (Will-
    iams).

51. PLACODIUM (DC.) Naeg. & Hepp.
    62. P. ELEGANS (Link.) D C. On stone. Pine Ridge, Aug. A very
    pretty orange red species, abundant in this region. (Webber).
    63. P. MICROPHYLLINUM Tuckerm. On old bark, Pine Ridge, Aug.
    (Webber).
    64. P. VITELLINUM (Ehrh.) Naeg. & Hepp. On sandstone. Lincoln,
    Sept. (Webber).

52. COLLEMA Hoffm., Fr.
    65. C. PULPOSUM (Bernh.) Nyl. On sandstone. Pine Ridge, Aug.
    (Webber).

53. PELTIGERA (Willd., Hoffm.) Fée.
    66. P. HORIZONTALIS (L.) Hoffm. On ground. Pine Ridge, Aug.
    (Webber.)

54. PHYSCIA (DC., Fr.) Th. Fr.
    67. P. HISPIDA (Schreb., Fr.) Tuckerm. On stone. Pine Ridge, Aug.
    (Webber).

55. PARMELIA (Ach.) De Not.
    68. P. MOLLIUSCULA Ach. On dry sterile soil, abundant. War Bonnet
    Canon, Harrison (Williams), Pine Ridge, Crawford (Webber).
    69. P. TILIACEA (Hoffm.) Floerk. var. SUB.LEVIGATA Nyl. On trees.
    Peru, Weeping Water (Williams).

14   *H. J. Webber —*

25. PEZIZACEÆ.

56. PEZIZA Fuckel.

70. P. HEMISPHÆRICA Wigg. Manure etc., Wabash (Williams).

26. UREDINEÆ

57. UROMYCES Link.

71. U. HOWEI Peck. On Milkweed (*Asclepias syriaca*), Fremont, July 31. Very destructive (Williams).

72. U. TRIFOLII (Alb. & Schw.) Winter. On red clover (*Trifolium pratense*), Ashland. Quite plentiful and somewhat destructive (Williams).

58. MELAMPSORA Cast.

73. M. LINI (DC.) Tul. On Wild-flax (*Linum perenne* var *lewisii*), Hat Creek Basin; Wild-flax (*Linum rigidum*), Weeping Water. Very destructive especially on the latter host. (Williams).

59. PUCCINIA Pers.

74. P. ANEMONES-VIRGINIANÆ Schw. On Long fruited anemone (*Anemone cylindrica*), Weeping Water. (Williams).

75. P. FUSCA Relhan. On Anemone, Ashland (Williams).

76. P. HYDROPHYLLI Peck & Cke. On leaves of Water leaf (*Hydrophyllum virginicum*) Sarpy Co. (Pound.)

77. P. MIRABILISSIMA Peck. II & III. On Barberry (*Berberis repens*), Belmont, July 24. The teleutospores are rarely found. In my Nebraska material I found but two. They, however, agree and compare well. (Webber).

78. P. SANICULÆ Grev. On Black snake root (*Sanicula canadensis*), Ashland (Williams).

79. P. SCIRPI DC. III On Bull-rush (*Scirpus* sp.), Lincoln, April (Webber).

80. P. SMILACIS Schw. On Greenbrier (*Smilax hispida*), Ashland. Abundant, causing the leaves to turn yellow and fall off (Williams).

60. PHRAGMIDIUM Link.

81. P. SUBCORTICIUM (Schrank.) Wint. Stage I on Rose (*Rosa arkansana*), Milford, May, 86; (Webber). Cultivated Rose (*Rosa* sp.), Lincoln, May (Webber). Weeping Water and Ashland (Williams).

This includes the specimens referred to stage II of *P. speciosum* (No. 416) in the catalogue, but does not include those of stage III.

On leaves petioles and stems, orange red, very conspicuous. Frequently quite injurious (Webber).

61. ÆCIDIUM Pers.

82. A. CALLIRRHOES Ell. & Kell. On *Malva* sp. Ashland (Williams).

83. A. MICROPUNCTUM E. & E. On Painted cup (*Castilleja sessiliflora* Pursh), Belmont, June 17. Quite destructive. (Williams.)

62. UREDO Pers.

84. U. RIBICOLA C. & E. On leaves of Buffalo or Missouri currant (*Ribes aureum*), Collected by Dr. Thomas in Scott's Bluff County.

Although determined to be a *Uredo* by Messrs. Cooke and Ellis (Grevillea VI, p. 86) and also by Peck who named it *Uredo jonesii* (Torr. Bull. XII, p. 36) it seems more like a *Coleosporium*, which it will probably turn out to be. All attempts at germinating the spores have thus far failed (Bessey).

27. USTILAGINEÆ.

63. USTILAGO Pers.

85. U. CARICIS (Pers.) Fckl. On Sedge (*Carex filifolia*) Sioux Co. June. Very plentiful, destroying the ovaries of nearly all the host plants in that vicinity. (Williams).

86. U. RABENHORSTIANA Kuhn. On finger grass (*Panicum sanguinale*) Ashland.

On flower spikes in the sheath, completely destroying them (spores brown, echinulate, round ellipsoid or angular, 7-12 by 8-13 m. m. m.). (Williams).

64. UROCYSTIS Rabenh.

87. U. OCCULTA (Wallr.) Rabenh. On Wild rye (*Elymus canadensis*), Ashland. (Williams).

28. EXOASCEÆ.

65. EXOASCUS Fuckel.

88. E. PRUNI Fckl. On common wild plum causing the disease known as "plum pockets." Weeping Water, quite common. (Williams), Dawes Co. (Bessey). On *Prunus pumila* at Long Pine (Bessey).

29. SACCHAROMYCETES.

66. SACCHAROMYCES Meyen.

89. S. MYCODERMA Reess. Lincoln (Pound).

30. SPHÆRIOIDEÆ.

67. PHYLLOSTICTA Pers.

90. P. CORNI West. On Red osier dogwood (*Cornus stolonifera*), Belmont, July (Webber.)

91. P. CRUENTA (Fr.) Kx. On False Solomon's seal (*Smilacina stellata*), Ashland (Williams); False Solomon's seal (*S. amplexicaulis*), New Helena, Custer Co., July 6. Frequently quite destructive. (Webber.)

92. P. PERSIC.E Sacc. On leaves of peach. Rock Creek and Ashland (Williams).

93. P. PIRINA Sacc. On apple leaves. Abundant and frequently destructive, Nov. 20. Lincoln. (Webber).

94. P. SEROTINA Cooke. On cherry (*Prunus serotina?*), Richardson Co., Aug. 25. Quite destructive in the locality where the specimens were collected. (Webber).

95. P. ULMICOLA Sacc. On Elm (*Ulmus americana*), Ashland, Oct. (Williams).

68. VERMICULARIA Fr.

96. V. LILIACEARUM Schw. On wild garlic (*Allium canadense*), Ashland (Williams).

69. SEPTORIA Fr.

97. S. BRUNELLÆ Ell. & Hals. On Self-heal (*Brunella vulgaris*), Richardson Co., Aug. 26 (Webber).

98. S. CEPHALANTHI Ell. & Kell. On leaves of Button bush (*Cephalanthus occidentalis*), West Point (Williams).

99. S. CORYLINA Peck. On Hazel nut (*Corylus americana*), Nebraska City, June. Not uncommon. (Webber).

100. S. LITTOREA Sacc. On Dogbane (*Apocynum cannabinum*), Elmwood, Weeping Water, Wabash (Williams).

101. S. RHOINA B. & C. On Sumach. (*Rhus glabra*), Nebraska City, June 1; Common, (Webber). Ashland and Weeping Water (Williams).

70. RHABDOSPORA Mont.

102. R. CONTINUA (B. & C.) Sacc. On stems of Plantain (*Plantago elongata*), Lincoln, March. Forming on old stems, numerous inconspicuous little black specks. (Webber).

31. LEPTOSTROMACEÆ.

71. LEPTOSTROMA, Fr.

103. L. SCIRPINUM Fr. On dead leaves of Riverrush (*Scirpus fluviatilis*), Weeping Water. (Williams.)

32. MELANCONIEÆ.

72. GLŒOSPORIUM Desm. & Mont.

104. G. SPHÆRELLOIDES Sacc. On *Hoya carnosa* in conservatory, Lincoln (Pound).

73. COLLETOTRICHUM Corda.

105. C. LINEOLA Corda. On leaves and culms of False red-top (*Eragrostis pectinacea*), Roca., Sept 22; Sand-bur (*Cenchrus tribuloides*), Lincoln Oct. 3, (Webber).

74. MELANCONIUM Link.

106. M. MAGNUM (Grev.) Berk. On dead Hickory, Ashland (Williams).

33. MUCEDINEÆ.

75. BOTRYTIS Mich.

107. B. CERATIOIDES Peck. On decaying boards, Weeping Water. (Williams).

76. RAMULARIA Ung.

108. R. DESMODII Cooke. On leaves of Tick-trefoil (*Desmodium canescens*), Weeping Water, Wabash, Ashland (Williams); Tick trefoil (*D. canadensis*), Lincoln, Aug. (Webber). In places very destructive.

109. R. IMPATIENTIS Peck. On leaves of Wild-balsam (*Impatiens fulva* and *I. pallida*), Ashland (Williams).

110. R. OCCIDENTALIS Ell. & Kell. On leaves of Dock (*Rumex altissimus*), Lincoln (Pound).

111. R. OXALIDIS Farlow. On leaves of Sorrel (*Oxalis violacea*), Ashland (Williams).

77. STACHYBOTRYS Corda.

112. S. LOBULATA Berk. On decaying broom, Lincoln (Pound).

34. DEMATIEÆ.

78. CERATOPHORUM Sacc.

113. C. ULMICOLUM Ell. & Kell. On leaves of American Elm (*Ulmus americana*), Ashland, October (Williams).

79. HELMINTHOSPORIUM Link.

114. H. LANCEOLATUM Cooke. Lincoln (Williams).

80. CERCOSPORA Fries.

115. C. ÆRUGINOSA Cooke. On leaves of Buckthorn (*Rhamnus lanceolatus*), Ashland (Williams).

116. C. DATURÆ Peck. On leaves of Stramonium (*Datura stramonium*), Ashland (Williams).

117. C. DUBIA (Riess) Wint. (*C. chenopodii* Fr.)
On Pigweed or goose-foot (*Chenopodium album*), Pine Ridge, July 29 (Webber).

118. C. ECHINOCYSTIS Ell. & Mart. On Wild cucumber (*Echinocystis lobata*), Waverly (Williams).

119. C. FLAGELLARIS Ell. & Mart. On Poke weed (*Phytolacca decandra*). Richardson Co. Aug. 1 (Webber).

120. C. GYMNOCLADI Ell. & Kell. On leaves of Kentucky Coffee tree (*Gymnocladus canadensis*), very common, Ashland (Williams); Richardson Co., Aug. (Webber).

121. C. LIPPLE Ell. & Ev. On leaves of *Lippia lanceolata*, Ashland. Quite destructive (Williams).

122. C. SAGITTARIÆ Ell. & Kell. On Arrow-head (*Sagittaria variabilis*), Weeping Water. (Williams.)

2

123. C. SYMPHORICARPI Ell. &. Ev.   On Indian Currant (*Symphoricar-pus vulgaris*), Rock Creek, July (Williams.)

124. C. VERNONIE Ell. & Kell.   On Iron weed (*Vernonia fasciculata*), Rock Creek, Wabash, Ashland. (Williams).   Very plentiful and quite destructive.

35. STILBEÆ.
81. ISARIA Pers.

125. I. SULPHUREA Fiedl.   On ground, Lincoln.   (Webber).

36. NIDULARIACEÆ.
82. CYATHUS Hall.

126. C. STRIATUS (Huds.) Hoffm.   On decaying matter.   Wabash, Ashland, Weeping Water.   (Williams).

37. LYCOPERDACEÆ.
83. GEASTER Mich.

127. G. HYGROMETRICUS Pers.   On ground, Pine Ridge, Dawes Co., July (Webber).

84. BOVISTA Dill.

128. B. SUBTERRANEA Peck.   Dismal River, Thomas Co., and Pine Ridge.   Very common in Central and Western regions.   This species is thought by many mycologists to be identical with *B. circumscissa*, B. & C. (No. 785 of the catalogue).   De Toni, (in Sacc. Syl. Fung.) keeps them distinct.   Mr. Morgan says he can easily distinguish between the two in the Nebraska material sent him, which, to my certain knowledge, was collected in similar localities.   For this reason I insert the species here, although, it is probably nothing more than a form of B. *circumscissa* B. & C. (Webber).

85. LYCOPERDON Tourn.

129. L. CURTISII Berk.   Lincoln.   (Webber).

130. L. WRIGHTII B. & C.   var. SEPARANS Peck.   On ground, Dismal River, Thomas Co., July 12; Pine Ridge, July 25   (Webber).

86. ARACHNION Schw.

131. A. ALBUM Schw.   On ground among weeds.   Lincoln, Aug. (Webber).

38. AGARICINEÆ.
87. LEPIOTA Fr.

132. L. OBLITA Peck.   Woods, Weeping Water, Lincoln.   Common, (Williams).

88. ARMILLARIA Fr.

133. A. MELLEA Vahl.   Base of stumps etc., common, Weeping Water (Williams).

89. TRICHOLOMA Fr.

134. T. TERREUM Schaeff.   Woods, Weeping Water.   (Williams).

90. CLITOCYBE Fr.

    135. C. INFUNDIBULIFORMIS Schaeff. Ashland, rare (Williams).

91. COLLYBIA Fr.

    136. C. VELUTIPES Curt. Bases of stumps of Hickory trees. Ashland, Weeping Water, common (Williams).

92. PLEUROTUS Fr.

    137. P. ULMARIUS Bull. Trunks of Elm, Boxelder, etc. Generally late in autumn, common. Lincoln, Ashland, Weeping Water (Williams).

93. LENTINUS Fr.

    138. L. LECOMTEI Fr. On old logs, especially Cottonwood. Weeping Water, Ashland, Wabash. Common, (Williams).

94. PLUTEUS Fr.

    139. P. CERVINUS Schaeff. On much decayed logs, common. Ashland. (Williams).

95. ENTOLOMA Fr.

    140. E. RHODOPOLIUM Fr. Moist woods. Ashland (Williams).

96. PHOLIOTA Fr.

    141. P. PRÆCOX Pers. Grassy places after rains. Lincoln, Weeping Water. (Williams).

97. HYPHOLOMA Fr.

    142. H. VELUTINUM Pers. Lincoln, Weeping Water (Williams).

39. POLYPOREÆ.

98. POLYPORUS Mich.

    143. P. ELEGANS (Bull.) Fr. On old wood, Lincoln. A very pretty species with somewhat excentric stipe about 1¾ in. long, thick pileus, and decurrent hymenium. Rare. (Webber).

40. HYDNEÆ.

99. HYDNUM L.

    144. H. CIRRATUM Pers. On old stump, Lincoln, June. Mr. Ellis writes — "Rare, I have it also from Iowa and New York." My only specimens were sent to Mr. Ellis for determination hence are in Herb. Ellis.

    Hymenium with very long coarse teeth, blue brown. (Webber).

100. IRPEX Fr.

    145. I. OBLIQUUS (Schrad.) Fr. On dead limbs of Elm, Ashland (Williams).

41. THELEPHOREÆ.

101. STEREUM Pers.

    146. S. NEGLECTUM Pk. (Rep. 33 p. 22.) On bark of trees, common. Lincoln (Webber).

42. CLAVARIEÆ.

102. PTERULA Fr.

    147. P. MULTIFIDA Fr. On decaying leaves at bases of trees in heavy timber, rare. Wabash (Williams).

43. TREMELLINEÆ.

103. GUEPINA Fr.

    148. G. SPATHULARIA (Schw.) Fr. On old boards, R. R. ties, etc., common. Weeping Water and Ashland (Williams). Lincoln (Webber).

44. CHAREÆ.

104. CHARA (Vaill.) Leonh.

    149. C. CONTRARIA A. Br. Flowing or standing water and cold springy lakes. Fremont, July (Williams).

    150. C. FRAGILIS, Desv. In ponds. Greeley Center, Greenwood, Fremont (Williams).

105. NITELLA Ag.

    151. N. ACUMINATA A. Br. var. GLOMERATA A. Br. Ponds near Lincoln (Bessey).

    152. N. FLEXILIS Ag. Ponds near Minden. In material collected by Dr. Hapeman (Bessey).

    153. N. MUCRONATA A. Br. Ponds near Minden. In material collected by Dr. Hapeman (Bessey).

BRYOPHYTA.

45. BRYACEÆ.

106. GYMNOSTOMUM Hedw.

    154. G. RUPESTRE Schwægr. (*Mollia æruginosa* (Sm.) Lindb.). On damp overhanging stone cliff. Pine Ridge, July 25 (Webber).

107. DICRANELLA Schimp.

    155. D. VARIA Schimp. On wet clayey soil, banks of the Mo. River. Peru, March (Webber).

108. DESMATODON Brid.

    156. D. ARENACEUS Sulliv. & Lesq. On ground. Collected by Mr. Brunner at Ashland, May (Webber).

    157. D. NERVOSUS. Bruch. & Schimp. var EDENTULUS Bruch. & Schimp. Abundant on stone. Peru, March (Webber).

109. BARBULA. Hedwig.

    158. B. RURALIS Hedw. Pine Ridge, Aug. 3 (Webber).

110. BRYUM Dill.

    159. B. CÆSPITICIUM L. Earth, Weeping Water (Williams).

111. ATRICHUM Beauv.

    160. A. PARALLELUM Mitt. Moist banks. Pine Ridge, June (Williams).

    161. A. ANGUSTATUM. Bruch. & Schimp. Long Pine (Bessey).

112. POLYTRICHUM L.

    162. P. JUNIPERINUM Wlld. On ground. Collected by Mr. Conklin at Long Pine (Webber).

113. HYPNUM Dill.

    163. H. FLUVIATILE Swartz. West Nebraska (Webber).

    164. H. RADICALE Beauv. On damp decaying log. Hat Creek Basin, Sioux Co. Aug. (Webber).

    165. H. RUTABULUM L. var. LONGISETUM Brid. Wet dripping banks and rocks, Ashland, April (Williams).

    166. H. SERRULATUM Hedw. On ground. Peru, March; Nebraska City, June (Webber).

PTERIDOPHYTA.

46. MARSILIACEÆ.

114. MARSILIA L.

    167. M. VESTITA Hook. & Grev. In ponds in many places in the State; Fairmont, Bradshaw, Minden, Geneva. Apparently not occurring east of the Blue River. The Fairmont specimens collected in 1890 agree with the variety *tenuifolia* in the hairiness, and shape of the leaflets, but nearly all the specimens collected this year (1891) fully agree with the specific characters of *M. vestita.* A few specimens were received which were more hairy, and whose leaflets were narrower, but upon investigation these were found to be terrestrial forms. In some cases these tenuifolia-like forms were connected directly with the larger smooth and broad leaved aquatic forms. The season of 1890 was a very dry one which probably accounts for the small size of the plants and the hairiness and narrow growth of the leaflets (Bessey).

47. FILICES.

115. CHEILANTHES Swz. Lip-fern.

    168. C. LANUGINOSA Nutt. Exposed rocks, two miles S. W. of Hackberry Springs, Banner Co. Aug. (Rydberg). Redwillow Co. (Bessey.)

ANTHOPHYTA.

48. NAIADACEÆ.

116. NAIAS L. Naiad.
> 169. N. FLEXILIS Rostk. & Schmidt. Stagnant water, Greenwood, July (Williams).

117. RUPPIA L. Ditch grass.
> 170. R. OCCIDENTALIS Watson. In Grand Lake (brackish water), abundant. Alliance Aug. 6. This is the form mentioned in the Catalogue under *Ruppia maritima* as probably belonging to the foreign variety *pedunculata* Hart. Mr. Morong writes: "There can be no doubt that the specimens sent me are *R. occidentalis* Watson, but with some differences. The leaves are somewhat shorter, the peduncles much longer and the fruit somewhat smaller. This form has not hitherto been found this side of Canada." (Webber.)

118. POTAMOGETON L. Pond weed.
> 171. P. AMPLIFOLIUS Tuckerm. Cropsey's Lake, Lincoln, July (Webber).
> 172. P. FLUITANS Roth. (*P. lonchites*, Tuckerm.). Streams, etc. Anselmo, Custer Co. July (Webber).
> 173. P. OAKESIANUS Robbins. In pond, Thedford, Thomas Co., July 11. A rare find. Mr. Morong writes — "It is the first time I have ever known this species to occur so far west. The most westerly locality known for it hitherto has been the Adirondack region in New York." (Webber.)
> 174. P. PECTINATUS L. Lakes, etc., abundant. Fremont, July (Williams). Grand Lake, Alliance, Aug.; Thedford, Thomas Co., Aug. (Webber).
> 175. P. SPIRILLUS Tuckerm. Lincoln, July (Webber).
> 176. P. ZOSTERÆFOLIUS Schum. Springy Lakes. Fremont, July; Greeley Center, July (Williams).

49. HYDROCHARIDACEÆ.

119. ELODEA Michx. Water-weed.
> 177. E. CANADENSIS Michx. Margins of Cold Lakes. Fremont, July (Williams).

50. ALISMACEÆ.

120. SAGITTARIA L. Arrow head.
> 178. S. CALYCINA Engelm. Moist Banks, Greenwood, July (Williams).
> 179. S. HETEROPHYLLA Pursh. Shallow water and muddy banks. Greenwood, July (Williams).

180. S. VARIABILIS Engelm. var. ANGUSTIFOLIA Engelm. Narrow leaves with very narrow diverging lobes. Lodge Pole Creek, Deuel Co., July (Rydberg). Thedford, Thomas Co., Aug. 7; Anselmo, Custer Co., July (Webber).

181. S. VARIABILIS Engelm. var. LATIFOLIA (Willd.) Engelm. With monœcious flowers, broad and acute leaves. Near Platte River, Kearney Co., Aug. (Rydberg). Lincoln, Aug. (Webber).

182. S. VARIABILIS Engelm. var. OBTUSA (Willd.) Engelm. With diœcious flowers and broad and obtuse leaves. Sand Creek below Wahoo, Sanders Co., Sept. (Rydberg).

51. TYPHACEÆ.

121. TYPHA L. Cat-tail flag.

183. T. LATIFOLIA L. var. TRIVIALE (Pursh) B. S. P. Common Cat-tail. Long Pine (Swezey).

52. CYPERACEÆ.

122. CAREX L. Sedge.

184. C. AUREA Nutt. Wooded cañons and low prairies, very common. Lewellen, Alliance (Swezey). Thedford, Thomas Co., July; Hat Creek Basin, Aug.; Pine Ridge, July (Webber).

185. C. DOUGLASII Boott. Dry prairies. Anselmo, Custer Co., July (Webber).

186. C. FILIFOLIA Nutt. Dry places. War Bonnet Cañon, June (Williams). Alliance (Swezey). Hitchcock Co. (Hapeman).

187. C. FILIFORMIS L. var. LATIFOLIA Boeckl. Crete, Alliance (Swezey). Ashland, War Bonnet Cañon (Williams). Pine Ridge, Anselmo, Thedford (Webber).

188. C. GRAVIDA Bailey, var. LAXIFOLIA Bailey. Broken Bow, July 4 (Webber).

189. C. LAXIFLORA Lam. var. VARIANS Bailey. Nebraska City, June 1 (Webber).

190. C. MARCIDA Boott. Dry prairies. Alliance (Swezey). Anselmo, Broken Bow, Thedford (Webber).

191. C. MUHLENBERGII Schkuhr. Low prairies. War Bonnet, Weeping Water, June–July (Williams).

192. C. PENNSYLVANICA Lam. Crete, common (Swezey).

193. C. SARTWELLII Dewey. Ashland, May (Williams).

194. C. SQUARROSA L. Lincoln (Webber).

195. C. STIPATA Muhl. Low prairies, common, Crete (Swezey), Thedford, July 10, Anselmo, July 5 (Webber).

196. C. STRAMINEA Schkr. var. BREVIOR Dewey. Elmwood, June (Williams); Anselmo, Custer Co., July (Webber).

197. C. TETANICA Schkr. Ashland, May (Williams).

198. C. TRIBULOIDES Wahl. var. CRISTATA (Schw.) Bailey. Low ground. Wabash, July 5 (Williams).

199. C. TRICHOCARPA Muhl. var. ARISTATA (R. Br.) Bailey.   Low prairies and moist places. Elmwood, Ashland (Williams).

123. HEMICARPHA Nees.

200. H. MICRANTHA (Vahl.) Britt. (*H. subsquarrosa* Nees.)   Minden. Collected by Dr. Hapeman (Bessey). Ashland (Williams).

124. ERIOPHORUM L. Cotton grass.

201. E. GRACILE Koch. Collected at Minden by Dr. Hapeman (Bessey).

125. FIMBRISTYLIS Vahl.

202. F. CAPILLARIS (L.) Gray. Long Pine (Swezey). Minden (Hapeman and Bessey).

203. F. CASTANEA Vahl. (*F. spadicea* Vahl. var. *castanea* Gray). Collected by Rev. Bates at Valentine (Rydberg). Minden (Hapeman).

126. HELEOCHARIS R. Br.

204. H. ATROPURPUREA (Retz.) Kunth. Collected by Dr. Wibbe in Filmore Co. Reported by Dr. Britton (Torr. Bull. Vol. XVIII, May, 1891, p. 166).

205. H. OVATA (Roth.) R. & S. var. ENGELMANNI (Stend.) Britt. Pine Ridge, June 18 (Williams).

206. H. PALUSTRIS (L.) Roem. & Schult. var. GLAUCESCENS (Willd.) Gray. Anselmo, Custer Co., July 6 (Webber).

127. DULICHIUM Pers.

207. D. SPATHACEUM (L.) Pers. Collected by Rev. Bates at Valentine, Aug. 14 (Rydberg).

128. CYPERUS L.

208. C. ACUMINATUS Torr. & Hook. Doniphan (Swezey). Lincoln, July 20 (Webber).

209. C. DIANDRUS Torr. Long Pine (Swezey).

210. C. DIANDRUS Torr. var. CASTANEUS Torr. Very abundant, Mo. River bottoms, Richardson Co., Aug. 26 (Webber).

211. C. STRIGOSUS L. Ravenna, Brewster, Long Pine (Swezey).

53. GRAMINEÆ.

129. ASPRELLA Willd.

212. A. HYSTRIX (L.) Willd. Roadsides N. E. of Wahoo, June (Rydberg).

130. ELYMUS L.   Wild Rye.

213. E. ELYMOIDES (Raf.) Swezey. (*E. sitanion* Schultes). Lewellen Swezey.

131. AGROPYRUM Gœrtn.   Wheat grass.

214. A. DASYSTACHYUM Vasey. Banks in thin woodlands; War Bonnet, June, 23. Rare (Williams).

132 BROMUS L.   Brome grass.
 215. B. CILIATUS L. var. PURGANS Gray. Belmont (Swezey).

133. GLYCERIA R. Br.   Manna grass.
 216. G. PALLIDA (Eddy) Trin. Wet places at margins of streams. War Bonnet, June 23. Rare (Williams).

134. POA L.   Meadow grass.
 217. P. ALSODES Gray. Woods on hillsides. War Bonnet, June (Williams).
 218. P. NEVADENSIS Vasey. Woods in War Bonnet cañon near edges of stream, June 21 (Williams).
 219. P. SYLVESTRIS Gray. Edges of woods, War Bonnet, June 23 (Williams).

135. DIPLACHNE Beauv.
 220. D. FASCICULARIS (Lam.) Beauv. Collected in Minden by Dr. Hapeman and in Rock Co., by Rev. Bates (Bessey). Greenwood (Williams).

136. AVENA L.   Oats.
 221. A. STRIATA Michx. Wild oats. War Bonnet, June (Williams).

137. ARISTIDA L.   Triple-awned grass.
 222. A. TUBERCULOSA Nutt. Collected at Minden by Dr. Hapeman (Bessey).

138. PANICUM L.   Panic-grass.
 223. P. WILCOXIANUM Vasey. Prairies Ft. Niobrara. First collected by Dr. T. E. Wilcox, the post surgeon, and by him submitted to Dr. Vasey who described it as new in Bull. 8, U. S. Dept. Agriculture (Botanical Division) 1889, p. 32.

 It is very near *Panicum scoparium* Lam. if indeed it is not a depauperate form of it (Bessey).

54.   JUNCACEÆ.

139. JUNCUS Tourn.   Rush, Bog-rush.
 224. J. BALTICUS Dethard var. MONTANUS Engelm. Alliance (Swezey). Broken Bow, July 4; Thedford, July 15 (Webber).
 225. J. BUFONIUS L. Sandy ground, not uncommon. Lawrence Fork, Banner Co., Aug. (Rydberg). Broken Bow, July 4; Thedford, July 12 (Webber).
 226. J. MARGINATUS Rostk. var. PAUCICAPITATUS Engelm. Brewster (Swezey).
 227. J. NODOSUS L. Low prairies and edges of streams, very common. Thedford, Thomas Co., July 14; Anselmo, July 6 (Webber). Long Pine (Swezey).
 228. J. TENUIS Willd. var. SECUNDUS Engelm. Long Pine (Swezey).

55.   LILIACE.E.

140. CALOCHORTUS Pursh.

    229. C. NUTTALLII Torr. & Gr.   Along sides of cañons.   Pine Ridge, June (Williams).

141. FRITILLARIA L.

    230. F. ATROPURPUREA Nutt.   Along sides of cañons.   War Bonnet, June (Williams).

142. POLYGONATUM Adans.   Solomon's seal.

    231. P. BIFLORUM (Walt.) Ell.   Cass Co (Williams).

143. SMILAX L.   Greenbrier, Catbrier.

    232. S. HERBACEA L. var PUBERULENTA Gray.   Woodlands, War Bonnet, June (Williams).

56.   IRIDACEÆ.

144. IRIS L.   Iris, Flag.

    233. I. VERSICOLOR L. Common Blue-flag.   Edges of ponds, etc., common.   Nebraska City, June (Webber).

57.   PONTEDERIACEÆ.

145. HETERANTHERA Ruiz & Pav.   Mud plantain.

    234. H. LIMOSA Vahl.   In ponds, common.   Lincoln and Fairmont (Bessey).   Minden (Hapeman).

58.   ORCHIDACEÆ.

146. HABENARIA Willd.ˑ   Rein orchis.

    235. H. BRACTEATA (Willd.) R. Br.   Moist places, common.   War Bonnet, June (Williams).

147. SPIRANTHES L.   Ladies' tresses.

    336. S. CERNUA (L.) Rich.   Sand flats, on islands of the Platte River near Ashland.   Sept. (Williams).

148. CORALLORHIZA R. Br.   Coral root.

    237. C. INNATA R. Br.   Damp dark woods in cañon.   War Bonnet, June (Williams).

    238. C. MULTIFLORA Nutt.   More common than the preceding species. Same locality (Williams).

59.   CUPULIFERÆ.

149. BETULA L.   Birch.

    239. B. PAPYRIFERA Marshall.   Paper or Canoe birch, White birch.   On the north slopes of the bluffs of the Niobrara River near Valentine (Bessey).

60. JUGLANDACEÆ.

150. HICORIA Raf.   Hickory.

240. H. SULCATA (Willd.) Britt.   Richardson Co. (Bessey).

61. SALICACEÆ.

151. SALIX L.   Willow, Osier.

241. S. ROSTRATA Richardson.   Wooded cañons, common. Belmont, July. Hat Creek Basin, Aug. (Webber).

242. S. TRISTIS Ait. Dwarf gray willow. An-elmo, Custer Co., July. Mr. Bebb writes: "This is the most westerly locality of this species known to me." (Webber). Long Pine (Bates).

62. CERATOPHYLLEÆ.

152. CERATOPHYLLUM L.   Hornwort.

243. C. DEMERSUM L. Shallow lakes. Fremont, Greenwood, Ashland. June–Sept. (Williams.)

63. POLYGONACEÆ.

153. RUMEX L.   Dock, Sorrel.

244. R. BRITANNICA L.   Long Pine (Swezey).

154. POLYGONUM L.   Knotweed, Smartweed.

245. P. HYDROPIPEROIDES Michx. Mild water-pepper. Wet places at edges of water, etc. Wabash, Aug. (Williams).

246. P. LAPATHIFOLIUM L.   Belmont (Swezey).

247. P. LAPATHIFOLIUM L. var INCARNATUM (Ell.) Watson.   Lawrence Fork, July 8 (Rydberg).

248. P. MUHLENBERGII Watson. Low places. Wabash, Weeping Water, Ashland, Aug.– Sept. (Williams). Horse Creek, Scott's Bluff Co., Aug. 1; Lodge Pole Creek near Kimball, Aug. 12 (Rydberg).

155. ERIOGONUM Michx.

249. E. ANNUUM Nutt. f. ——. Sand hills Kearney Co. (Rydberg). Ewing (Bessey).

Of the *E. annuum* type but differing in size, being larger (2–3 ft.); naked above; leaves lanceolate, 2–2½ in. long, ½ in. wide, the upper nearly sessile; bracts triangular; flowers larger than those of *E. annuum*; the dense appressed woolliness turning yellowish on the branches (Rydberg).

250. E. BREVICAULE Nutt. Hills, Kiwa Valley, Scott's Bluff Co., July 28 (Rydberg).

251. E. CERNUUM Nutt. Court House Rock, July 4; Wild Cat Mountains, Banner Co., July 16; Scott's Bluff, July 25; hills near Kimball, Aug. 12; near Sidney, Aug. 16 (Rydberg).

252. E. CORYMBOSUM Benth. Sand draws of Cheyenne Co., Aug. (Rydberg).

253. E. MICROTHECUM Nutt. var. EFFUSUM (Nutt.) Torr. & Gr. Lodge Pole Creek (Swezey).

64. CHENOPODIACEÆ.

156. SUÆDA Forskal.   Sea blite.

254. S. PROSTRATA Pallas. (Ill. Pl. Imp. Cogn. p. 55 t. 47.— 1803). (*Salsola depressa*, Pursh Fl. 1814; Watson, in King's Rep.) Salt Creek Basin N. W. of Lincoln (Rydberg). Differs from *S. linearis* (Ell.) Torr. in having the leaves broadest at the base and one or more of the calyx lobes strongly carinate.

157. EUROTIA Adans.

255. E. LANATA (Pursh) Moq. White sage. Dry prairies, in "Bad lands," etc. Hat Creek Basin, Aug. (Webber). Hillsides, Pumpkin Seed Valley and Lawrence Fork (Rydberg).

A white tomentose undershrub of the aspect of an *Artemisia*. The margins of the leaves are revolute, which separates it at a glance from *Artemisia cana* which it otherwise resembles. It is known under the name of " White sage."

In Coulter's Manual *Eurotia* is described as diœcious. Watson in his "Revision of N. A. *Chenopodiaceæ*," states that it is sometimes monœcious, which is the case with all specimens found here (Rydberg).

158. ATRIPLEX L.

256. A. ARGENTEA Nutt. Not uncommon in the Salt Basin, N. W. of Lincoln, and saline soil in Kiwa Valley, Scott's Bluff Co. (Rydberg).

257. A. HORTENSIS L. Escaped along roads, etc. Hastings, Aug. 2 (Webber.)

159. MONOLEPIS Schrad.

258. M. CHENOPODIOIDES Moq. Dry saline soil in Deuel Co., June 27 (Rydberg).

160. CHENOPODIUM L.   Pigweed, Goosefoot.

259. C. BOSCIANUM Moq. Long Pine, Belmont (?) (Swezey); Bennett, Aug. (Webber.)

260. C. FREMONTII Watson. Collected by Rev. Bates at Alliance (Rydberg); Belmont (Swezey); Anselmo (Webber).

261. C. FREMONTII Watson. var. INCANUM Watson. Collected by Rev. Bates at Valentine (Rydberg). Dry prairies, very abundant in Prairie dog towns, Thedford, July 16 (Webber). Lawrence fork, July 8; Kiwa Valley, Scott's Bluff Co., Aug. 1 (Rydberg).

262. C. LEPTOPHYLLUM Nutt. Common in Central and Western Nebraska. Valentine (Bates). Lodge Pole Creek (Swezey).

Sandy soil, Kearney Co. (Rydberg). Thedford and Anselmo, July (Webber).

263. C. LEPTOPHYLLUM Nutt. var. OBLONGIFOLIUM Watson. Valentine, collected by Rev. Bates; also in broken soil, Deuel Co., July 12 (Rydberg).

264. C. LEPTOPHYLLUM Nutt. var. SUBGLABRUM Watson. Alliance (Swezey). Pine Ridge (Webber). Scott's Bluff, July 24 (Rydberg).

65. AMARANTACEÆ.

161. FRŒLICHIA Moench.

265. F. GRACILIS Moq. "Sand draws," Deuel Co., Aug. 24 (Rydberg).

66. CARYOPHYLLACEÆ.

(Including *Illecebraceæ.*)

162. CERASTIUM L.　　Mouse-ear, Chickweed.

266. C. ARVENSE L. Collected by Rev. Bates at Ft. Robinson (Bessey). War Bonnet Cañon (Williams).

267. C. VULGATUM L. Crete. (Swezey.)

163. STELLARIA L.　　Chickweed.

268. S. LONGIFOLIA Muhl. Long-leaved Stitchwort. Low wet banks. Dismal River, Thomas Co., July 12 (Webber).

164. ARENARIA L.　　Sandwort.

269. A. HOOKERI Nutt. Pine Ridge, July; Hat Creek Basin, Aug. High rocky places, very common.

Dr. Britton after comparison with Nuttall's type of this species refers to it all of my specimens reported in the catalogue as *Arenaria pungens* (Catalogue No. 1213).

Mr. Rydberg has sent me specimens of an *Arenaria* from the cliffs of a cañon in Banner Co., labeled *A. franklini* Dougl. var. *minor* Hook. & Arn. that is probably to be referred here also (Webber).

264½. LOEFLINGIA L.

270. L. SQUARROSA Nutt. High rocky prairies, Belmont, July 18. (Determined by Dr. Britton).

This is a very northerly locality for this plant, its usual range being from Southern California to Texas (Webber).

165. LYCHNIS L.　　Cockle.

271. L. DRUMMONDII Wat-on. Dry prairies. Hat Creek Basin, common, June (Williams).

272. L. GITHAGO (L.) Lam. Corn cockle. In cultivated fields. Weeping Water (Williams).

166. SILENE L.   Catchfly, Campion.

    273. S. MENZIESII Hook. Woodlands, common. War Bonnet, June (Williams).

    274. S. SCOULERI Hook. Pine Ridge, July (Webber).

167. SAPONARIA L. Soap-wort, Bouncing Bet.

    275. S. VACCARIA L. Crete (Swezey).

168. ANYCHIA Rich.   Forked chickweed.

    276. A. CANADENSIS (L.) B. S. P. (*A. dichotoma* Michx. var. *capillacea* Torr.) Woods, Weeping Water, June. Rare (Williams).

67. FICOIDEÆ.

(Luerssen places this under the family *Aizoaceœ*.)

169. MOLLUGO L.   Indian chickweed.

    277. M. VERTICILLATA L. Long Pine (Swezey). Minden (Hapeman). Deuel Co. (Rydberg).

68. BERBERIDACEÆ.

170. CAULOPHYLLUM Michx.   Pappoose-root.

    278. C. THALICTROIDES (L.) Michx. Blue cohosh. Sarpy Co., May (Pound).

69. RANUNCULACEÆ.

171. DELPHINIUM L.   Larkspur.

    279. D. TRICORNE Michx. Dwarf larkspur. Edges of woods. Elmwood, May–June (Williams).

172. RANUNCULUS L.   Buttercup, Crowfoot.

    280. R. CIRCINATUS Sibth. Lodge Pole Creek, Cheyenne Co., Aug. 19 (Rydberg).

    281. R. HISPIDUS Hook. Irrigated meadow north of Kimball, Aug. 12 (Rydberg).

70. CRUCIFERÆ.

173. THELYPODIUM Endl.

    282. T. INTEGRIFOLIUM Endl. Fields, etc., not uncommon. Alliance (Swezey). Pine Ridge, July 20 (Webber).

174. ERYSIMUM L.   Treacle mustard.

    283. E. ASPERUM DC. Sandy hills in Deuel Co., July. Collected also by Rev. Bates at Valentine.

        Pods widely spreading. Large specimens were observed to roll before the wind, thus adding another " Tumble weed " to the already long list (Rydberg).

175. PHYSARIA Nutt.

    284. P. DIDYMOCARPA Gray. Cañon south of Scott's Bluff, July 22 (Rydberg).

176. LESQUERELLA Watson.

285. L. ENGELMANNI (Gray) Watson. Lawrence Fork, Kimball Co., Aug. 11 (Rydberg).

286. L. GRACILIS (Hook.). Watson. Waste ground along railroad. Weeping Water, June.

This is quite a northern extension of its range. It may have been introduced through the agency of the R. R., being found only in this one place. It was, however, abundant and evidently spreading (Webber).

177. CARDAMINE L. Bitter cress.

287. C. LACINIATA (Muhl.) Wood. (*Dentaria laciniata* Muhl.) Peru. Communicated by Mr. A. H. Van Fleet (Bessey).

178. ARABIS L. Rock cress.

288. A. DENTATA (Torr.) Torr. & Gr. Low ground, rare. Lincoln, April (Webber).

289. A. GLABRA (L.) Bernh. (*A. perfoliata Lam.*). Tower mustard. Dismal River, Thomas Co., July (Webber).

290. A. HOLBŒLLII Hornem. Wooded cañons. Pine Ridge, June (Williams). Pumpkin Seed Valley, July 14 (Rydberg).

179. NASTURTIUM R. Br. Water cress.

291. N. OBTUSUM. Nutt. Ft. Clark, Nebraska (Hayden in Engelmann Herb.), Crete (Swezey), Minden (Hapeman), Big Springs (Rydberg).

Prof. Swezey's specimens differ somewhat from typical *N. obtusum*, being less diffusely spreading and branched, approaching likely nearer *N. sinuatum*. Hayden's specimens seem typical (Webber).

292. N. PALUSTRE (L.) DC. var. OVALE M. In mud, Sand Creek, Wahoo, Sept.

A small plant with the leaves entire, obovate or oval, crenate or with a pair or two of small lobes at the base; pod oval. (Rydberg.)

293. N. SESSILIFLORUM Nutt. Crete (Swezey). Wahoo Creek below Wahoo, Sept. (Rydberg). Lincoln, May (Webber).

294. N. SINUATUM Nutt. Moist places along banks, Elmwood, June (Williams), Fairbury (in Herb. Univ. of Nebr.). Omaha and Crete (Swezey). Platte River, Kearney Co., June 15 (Rydberg). Lincoln, May; Nebraska City, June (Webber). Pods and pedicels variously curved, forming a conspicuous character.

71. CAPPARIDACEÆ.

180. CRISTATELLA Nutt.

295. C. JAMESII Torr. and Gr. Collected by Rev. Bates at Valentine, Aug. 1 (Rydberg).

72. HYPERICACEÆ.

181. HYPERICUM L.   St. John's-wort.

296. H. CANADENSE L. Common in low grounds. Thedford, July 14 (Webber). Ashland (Williams). *H. mutilum L.* of Swezey's Nebr. Fl. Plants p. 5, is probably to be referred here.

297. H. CANADENSE L. var. MAJUS Gray. Wet Meadows. Saunders Co., June (Rydberg). Lowell, July 11 (Webber).

298. H. VIRGINICUM L. (*Elodes virginica* Nutt. and *E. campanulata* Pursh). Antelope Co. (Webber).

73. GERANIACEÆ.

182. ERODIUM L' Her.   Storksbill.

299. E. CICUTARIUM (L.) L'Her. Alfilaria. Lincoln. Along sidewalks, probably introduced in hay. Adventive from Europe (Williams).

74. LINACEÆ.

183. LINUM L.   Flax.

300. L. RIGIDUM Pursh. Prairie flax. Very common on the prairies of central and western Nebraska. Superior, Brewster, Long Pine, Lewellen (Swezey); Deuel Co., July (Rydberg); Thedford, July 14; Anselmo, July; Broken Bow, July; Belmont, Aug. (Webber).

A form collected at Hat Creek Basin Aug. 2, Prof. Trelease notes as having the habit of var. *puberulum* Engelm. (Webber).

301. L. USITATISSIMUM L. Cultivated Flax. Escaped to low prairies. Broken Bow, July (Webber).

75. SAPINDACEÆ.

184. ÆSCULUS L. Horse-chestnut, Buckeye.

302. A. GLABRA Willd. Richardson and Pawnee counties (Bessey).

76. EUPHORBIACEÆ.

185. EUPHORBIA L.   Spurge.

303. E. CUPHOSPERMA (Engelm.) Boiss. A few specimens collected Aug., 1890, in a cañon running north from Lawrence Fork, Banner Co.

Leaves lance linear, entire or with a few teeth on the revolute margin. Seeds short, triangular, truncate at the base, wrinkled and tuberculate, with a minute caruncle. Belongs to the *E. heterophylla* group (Rydberg).

304. E. FENDLERI Torr. & Gr. " Sand draw," Cheyenne Co., Aug.

The seeds are described in Coulter's Manual as irregularly punctate. In the original description in Pacific R. R. Rep. it reads " a little rugose transversely," which agrees with Nebraska specimens (Rydberg).

305. E. GEYERI Engelm. Collected by Rev. Bates at Valentine, July 1 (Rydberg).

77. UMBELLIFERÆ.

186. BERULA Koch.

306. B. ANGUSTIFOLIA (L.) Koch. In water, Hackberry Springs, Banner Co., Aug. (Rydberg); Long Pine, Lewellen, Belmont (Swezey); Anselmo, Thedford, July–Aug. (Webber).

187. CYMOPTERUS Raf.

307. C. GLOMERATUS Raf. Lewellen, Alliance (Swezey). Collected by Rev. Bates at Valentine, May (Rydberg).

188. PASTINACA L. Parsnip.

308. P. SATIVA L. Common parsnip. Introduced. Mead, Saunders Co., June, 1890 (Rydberg).

78. ARALIACEÆ.

189. ARALIA L. Wild sarsaparilla.

309. A. RACEMOSA L. Spikenard. Nebraska City, Aug. (Williams).

79. SAXIFRAGACEÆ.

190. RIBES L. Currant, Gooseberry.

310. R. GRACILE Michx. Wild gooseberry. Saunders Co. This is the common wild gooseberry of Saunders Co., and Eastern Nebraska. It differs from *R. rotundifolium* Michx. in having long and slender peduncles, and capillary filaments 4–6″ long. The majority of Nebraska specimens referred to *R. rotundifolium* Michx. likely belong here (Rydberg).

80. CACTACEÆ.

191. OPUNTIA Tourn.

311. O. RUTILA Nutt. Prairies. Deuel Co., June 23 (Rydberg).

81. ONAGRACEÆ.

192. OENOTHERA L. Evening primrose.

312. OE. ALBICAULIS Nutt. var. RUNCINATA Engelm. "Sand draws," Deuel Co., Aug. (Rydberg). Very likely this is the sinuate leaved form of *OE. albicaulis* referred to in the Catalogue Fl. Nebr. No. 1404.

313. OE. BIENNIS L. var. PARVIFLORA Gray. Petals hardly ½ in. long. Hills, Deuel Co. (Rydberg).

314. OE. HARTWEGII Benth. var. LAVANDULEFOLIA (Torr. & Gr.) Watson. Prairies, etc. Lisbon, Perkins Co., June 23; Deuel Co., June 27 and July 2: Pleasant Valley, Scott's Bluff Co., July 28; Banner Co., Aug. (Rydberg). Lewellen, rare (Swezey).

315. OE. SPECIOSA Nutt. Lincoln, probably an escape from cultivation (Bessey).

193. EPILOBIUM L.   Willow herb.
 316. E. HORNEMANNI Richenb. Belmont (Swezey). (*E. alpinum* L. of
   Swezey's Nebr. Fl. Plants, p. 8.) Its occurrence needs confirmation.

82. ROSACEÆ.

194. POTENTILLA L.   Five-finger.
 317. P. ANSERINA L. Silver-weed. Lewellen (Swezey).
 318. P. RIVALIS Nutt. var. PENTANDRA (Engelm.) Watson. Wabash,
   July (Williams).
 319. P. SUPINA L. Omaha, Lewellen (Swezey).

195. CERCOCARPUS H. B. K.   Mt. Mahogany.
 320. C. PARVIFOLIUS Nutt. Rocky hills, Banner Co., Aug. A shrub
   3–6 ft. high. Seen at a distance it gives the hills a peculiar dark
   grayish color caused partly by the beautiful plumy tails of the
   fruit (Rydberg).

83. LEGUMINOSÆ.

196. AMPHICARPÆA Ell.
 321. A. PITCHERI Torr. & Gr. Banks of Sand Creek below Wahoo,
   Sept. (Rydberg). Woods, Ashland (Williams).
   Leaflets larger than in *A. comosa*; rachis villous; bracts large,
   silky canescent; upper flowers commonly fertile (Rydberg).

197. LATHYRUS L.
 322. L. ORNATUS Nutt. . Differs from *L. polymorphus* in having linear
   lanceolate leaves and the seed with a broad stalk and long hilum
    Pierce, Ft. Robinson (Herb. Univ. of Nebr.), Phelps Co., Fre-
   mont (Rydberg).
   A light yellow form of *L. ornatus Nutt.* is also sometimes found, .
   Collected by Miss H. G. Wilkenson at Gordon. Fremont (Rydberg).

198. ASTRAGALUS L. Rattle-weed.
 323. A. CHAMÆLUCE(?) Gray. Alliance, Lewellen(Swezey, Nebr. Flowering Plants, p. 7).
   (The specimens differ from typical *A. chamæluce* in having too
   small flowers and too many leaflets. More abundant material is
   necessary to satisfactorily place the species. — Webber.)
 324. A. PICTUS Gray. var. FILIFOLIUS Gray. Lewellen, rare; Alliance
   (Swezey). Collected by Rev. Bates at Valentine (Rydberg) .

199. PETALOSTEMON Michx.   Prairie clover.
 325. P. COMPACTUS (Spreng.) Swezey. (*P. macrostachyus* Torr.)
   Lewellen (Swezey).
 326. P. TENUIFOLIUS Gray. "Sand draws," Deuel Co., July.
   Low, branching from below, decumbent; leaflets 1-2 pairs,

linear-filiform, revolute; bracts ovate, densely villous, as is also the calyx, with grayish, slightly tawny hairs (Rydberg).

327. P. sp.——. *P. candidus* var. *occidentalis* Gr. of Pringle's collection, according to Dr. Britton. It is, however, clearly no variety of *P. candidus*, but may be of *P. gracilis*, Nutt., of the south, to which it is nearly related. It differs from *P. gracilis* in having more oblong leaves, longer more lax spikes, and glandular dotted calyx. Dr. Britton says if distinct from *P. gracilis* it is clearly a distinct species (Rydberg).

200. PSORALEA L.   Psoralea.

328. P. DIGITATA Nutt. Aurora (Williams). Much confounded with *P. campestris.* Specimens in the Herb. of Univ. of Nebr. collected at Anselmo by Webber and at Valentine by Rev. Bates, evidently belong here. Nebraska specimens collected by Dr. Bessey, have been referred to *P. digitata* by Dr. Britton (Rydberg).

329. P. FLORIBUNDA Nutt. This species, I think, should not be merged into *P. tenuiflora* Pursh. It is either a distinct species or a well marked variety. *P. floribunda* Nutt. found in eastern Nebraska has generally 5 oblong leaflets, 1-1½ in. long; many flowered racemes; lower calyx teeth longer; and larger flowers. *P. tenuiflora* Pursh, of western Nebraska, has 3 oblong-oblanceolate leaflets, ½-¾ in. long; few flowered racemes; and punctate, colored calyx with equal teeth. Dr. Britton, to whom specimens and my notes upon them have been sent says: " I had concluded that *P. floribunda* could not go unnoticed into *P. tenuiflora*." The matter needs more investigation. Most of the localities for *P. tenuiflora* in the catalogue of Nebr. Flora belong to *P. floribunda.* The only specimens of the true *P. tenuiflora* I have seen are those collected by Dr. Bessey, at Ft. Robinson, and my own, from the plains of Deuel Co., Aug. 1890 (Rydberg).

330. P. HYPOGÆA Nutt. Alliance, Lewellen (Swezey). Hills, Deuel Co., June 26 (Rydberg).

331. P. LINEARIFOLIA Torr. & Gr. Magnesia cliffs in Deuel Co., July. Racemes very loose, 3-6 in. long; leaflets 3, linear, 1-2 in. long; stem, leaves, and calyx glandular dotted (Rydberg).

201. TRIFOLIUM L.   Clover, Trefoil.

332. T. PROCUMBENS L. Low hop-clover. Yards and roadsides, Lincoln. Adventive from Europe (Webber).

202. LUPINUS L.   Lupine.

333. L. ARGENTEUS Pursh var. ARGOPHYLLUS Watson. Prairies, rare. War Bonnet, June (Williams).

334. L. ARGENTEUS Pursh var. DECUMBENS Watson. "Sand draws," 2 miles S. W. of Hackberry Springs, Aug. (Rydberg). Prairies of Hat Creek Basin, common (Webber).

335. L. PUSILLUS Pursh. Lewellen (Swezey). Hills near Curtis, Frontier Co., June 23; Deuel Co., June 25 (Rydberg).

84. ERICACEÆ.

203. MONOTROPA L.   Indian pipe, Corpse-plant.

336. M. UNIFLORA L.   Washington and Cass Counties (Bessey).

204. PYROLA Tourn.   Wintergreen, Shin-leaf.

337. P. CHLORANTHA Sw. Damp dark wooded cañons, rare. War
Bonnet, June (Williams).

338. P. SECUNDA L.   Damp cañon at head of Jim Creek, Pine Ridge,
June 25. Very rare (Williams).

205. ARCTOSTAPHYLOS Adans.   Bearberry.

339. A. UVA-URSI (L.) Spreng. In a cañon near Anselmo, Custer
County. The occurrence of this plant in the center of the state,
hundreds of miles from any of its known stations, adds another
puzzle to the many connected with the geographical distribution
of the plants of the plains. It is known to occur in the Black
Hills of South Dakota and the Rocky Mountains in Wyoming and
Colorado. In Minnesota it is found near Pepin; it is absent from
Iowa, while in Missouri it is confined to the southeastern part.
It is doubtfully reported as occurring in Kansas. That it should
be found in Central Nebraska is certainly unexpected (Bessey).

85. PRIMULACEÆ.

206. CENTUNCULUS Dill.   Chaffweed.

340. C. MINIMUS L.   Fairfield (Swezey).

207. LYSIMACHIA Tourn.   Loosestrife.

341. L. THYRSIFLORA L. Tufted loosestrife. Collected by Rev. Bates
at Valentine, June (Rydberg); Lewellen (Swezey); Platte River
near Doniphan, May (Harvey Thompson).

208. DODECATHEON L.   American cowslip.

342. D. MEADIA L. Shooting-star. Alliance (Swezey).

86. CONVOLVULACEÆ.

209. CUSCUTA L.   Dodder, Love-vine.

343. C. TENUIFLORA Engelm. Crete, on *Salix* (Swezey).

210. CONVOLVULUS L.   Bindweed.

344. C. ARVENSIS L. Bindweed. Roadsides. Ashland, May (Williams).

87. POLEMONIACEÆ.

211. GILIA Ruiz & Pav.

. 345. G. GRACILIS Hook. " Sand draws " in Deuel Co., June 25 (Rydberg). War Bonnet Cañon (Williams).

346. G. LINEARIS (Nutt.) Gray. Sides of cañon, Squaw Creek, June

(Williams). Dry banks, common: Pine Ridge, July 18; Hat Creek Basin, Aug. 1 (Webber). "Sand draws" in Deuel Co., June 25 (Rydberg).

347. G. MINIMA Gray. Collected at Rushville, in July, by Rev. Bates (Rydberg).

348. G. PUNGENS Benth. var CAESPITOSA Gray. Hills in Kiwa Valley, July 22; Scott's Bluff, July 25 (Rydberg).

88. HYDROPHYLLACEÆ.

212. PHACELIA Juss.

349. P. CIRCINATA (Willd.) Jacq. Abundant in dry cañons. Pine Ridge, July (Webber). War Bonnet (Williams).

Very *Krynitzkia* like in appearance. Venation prominent above and below, leaf pinnately and obliquely straight veined. Lower leaves seldom with lateral leaflets in Nebraska specimens (Webber).

89. BORRAGINACEÆ.

213. LITHOSPERMUM L.   Gromwell, Puccoon.

350. L. LATIFOLIUM Michx.   Superior (Swezey).

351. L. PILOSUM Nutt.   War Bonnet, June (Williams).

214. MERTENSIA Roth.

352. M. LANCEOLATA (Pursh) DC.   Wooded cañons.   War Bonnet, June (Williams).

(Prof. Swezey's specimens from Lewellen and Chadron referred to this species, Nebr. Flowering Plants, p. 11, must be considered as belonging to *Pentstemon cæruleus* Nutt.—Webber.)

215. CRYPTANTHE Lehmann. [*Krynitzkia crassisepala* Gray and *K. glomerata* Gray, No's. 1577 and 1578 of the Catalogue of Neb. Flora, should be changed according to Prof. Greene's paper (Pittonia, I. p. 110–112) to *Cryptanthe glomerata* Lehmann and *C. crassisepala* (T. & G.) Greene.]

353. C. FENDLERI (Gr.) Greene l. c. (*Krynitzkia fendleri* Gray). Dry cañons, etc. "Bad lands." Hat Creek Basin, Sioux Co., Aug. (Webber). Lodge Pole Creek (Swezey). Collected by Rev. Bates at Harrison, Aug. Wild Cat Mts., Banner Co., July 17 (Rydberg).

216. OREOCARYA Greene. Pittonia I. p. 57.

354. O. FULVOCANESCENS (Gray) Greene, l. c. (*Krynitzkia fulvocanescens* Gray). Dry sterile places, War Bonnet, June (Williams); Hat Creek Basin, Aug. (Webber).

355. O. SUFFRUTICOSA (Torr.) Greene, l. c. (*Eritrichium jamesii* Torr. *Krynitzkia jamesii* (Torr.) Gray). Quite common in the western part of the state. Alliance (Swezey); Deuel Co.; Lawrence

Fork, Banner Co., Aug. (Rydberg); Harrison (Bates); Belmont, July; Hat Creek Basin, Aug. (Webber).

217. ECHINOSPERMUM Swartz.   Stickseed.

    356. E. DEFLEXUM (Wahl.) Lehm. var. AMERICANUM Gray. Long Pine (Swezey).

    357. E. FLORIBUNDUM Lehm. Lawrence Fork, Banner Co., July 17 (Rydberg).

90. SOLANACEÆ.

218. PHYSALIS L.   Ground cherry.

    358. P. LANCEOLATA Michx. var. HIRTA Gray. Prairies. Hat Creek Basin, June (Williams).

    Mr. Rydberg has noted two forms or varieties of *Physalis* belonging to the *lanceolata* group but differing enough from *P. lanceolata* to be distinct. I give below his descriptions in brief:—

    No. 1. Glabrous or minutely hirsute on the calyx and the angles of the stems, erect, branched above; corolla yellowish with darker spot, only 5-7 lines across; anthers yellow; fruiting calyx inversely pear shaped; fruit greenish yellow; leaves lanceolate, sparingly toothed. "Sand draws," Deuel and Banner Co.'s July, 1890 (Rydberg).

    No. 2. Slender, ascending; leaves oblong, lanceolate to oblanceolate, entire; calyx hispid; corolla, anthers, and fruit like the preceding; fruiting calyx globose. Near Pumpkin Seed Creek, Banner Co., Aug. 1890 (Rydberg).

91. SCROPHULARIACEÆ.

219 PEDICULARIS L.   Louse wort.

    359. P. CANADENSIS L. Bottom lands, common. Ashland, May (Williams).

    360. P. LANCEOLATA Michx. Moist woods, rare. Ashland. Sept. (Williams).

220. GERARDIA L.   Gerardia.

    361. G. TENUIFOLIA Vahl. var. MACROPHYLLA Benth. Dry woods, common. Ashland, Weeping Water (Williams).

221. LIMOSELLA L.   Mudwort.

    362. L. AQUATICA L. Spring in Deuel Co., June 27 (Rydberg).

222. MIMULUS L.   Monkey flower.

    363. M. LUTEUS L. Lewellen (Swezey).

223. PENTSTEMON Mitchell.   Beard tongue.

    364. P. HAYDENI Watson. (Bot. Gazette, XVI (Nov., 1891), p. 311) Sandy prairies in central Nebraska, quite common. It is frequently found in the edges of "blow outs." Antelope Co.) July; Dismal River, Thomas Co., July 12 (Webber).

This includes *Pentstemon glaber* Pursh var *utahensis* Watson, of Swezey's Nebr. Fl. Plants, p. 12; from Lewellen.

The habit is rather peculiar, growing as it does in very loose sandy places, the sand blowing here and there frequently banking up around it, modifies leaves and stems already formed. It is usually ascending, the lower portion of the stem running for some distance under the loose sand with no modification except a reduction of the leaves from lanceolate to linear and finally to filiform, or to mere scales. Many of the linear ones are quite long and expand somewhat above if the surface is reached (Webber).

92. OROBANCHACEÆ.

224. APHYLLON Mitchell.   Cancer root, Naked broom rape.

305. A. FASCICULATUM Gray. var. LUTEUM Gray. Collected by Rev. Bates at Valentine, June 10. Hills south of Scott's Bluff, July 26 (Rydberg).

93. LABIATÆ.

225. STACHYS L.   Hedge-nettle.

306. S. ASPERA Michx. var. TENUIFLORA (Willd.) Hitchcock, Cat. Anth. & Pter. of Ames, Ia., p. 513. (*Stachys aspera* Michx, var. *glabra* Gray). Banks of Wahoo Creek, Saunders Co., Aug. (Rydberg.)

307. S. PALUSTRIS L. Collected by Rev. Bates at Valentine (Rydberg); Kearney, June (Webber).

226. PHYSOSTEGIA Benth.   False dragon-head.

308. P. PARVIFLORA Nutt. Spring near Horse Creek, Scott's Bluff Co. Aug. 1 (Rydberg).

227. SCUTELLARIA L.   Skullcap.

309. S. GALERICULATA L. Lewellen (Swezey). Spring, near Horse Creek, Scott's Bluff Co., Aug. 1 (Rydberg).

228. MONARDA L.   Horse-mint.

370. M. FISTULOSA L. var MOLLIS (L.) Benth. Wild bergamot. Banks of ravines, etc., Wahoo, Aug. (Rydberg).

229. SALVIA L.   Sage.

371. S. AZUREA Lam. var. GRANDIFLORA Benth. Crete (Swezey).

230. MENTHA L.   Mint.

372. M. CANADENSIS L. var. BOREALIS (Michx) Wood. (*M. canadensis* L. var. *glabrata* Benth.) Remarkable for its sweet scent. Hackberry Springs, Banner Co., Aug. (Rydberg). Cass Co. (Williams).

373. M. SATIVA L. Whorled mint. River banks, rare. Fremont, July (Williams).

94. VERBENACEÆ.

231. VERBENA L.   Vervain.

> 374. V. BRACTEOSA x HASTATA. In a pasture 1 mile W. of Mead, Saunders Co., in June, 1890, there were found a few specimens of a Verbena, which undoubtedly is a hybrid between *V. bracteosa* Michx. and *V. hastata* L. The specimens are of the size and general appearance of *V. hastata*, but branched from the base and ascending. The leaves are of the size of those of *V. hastata* but more divided like those of *V. bractcosa*. The bracts are like those of the latter. Dr. Engelmann mentions several Verbena hybrids but not this (Rydberg).

> 375. V. OFFICINALIS L. Cultivated grounds and pastures, Wabash, July. Adventive from Europe (Williams). Tecumseh (Bessey).

232. LIPPIA L.

> 376. L. LANCEOLATA Michx. Low meadows, Ashland, July-Aug. Common (Williams). Richardson Co., Aug. (Webber). Minden (Bessey).

95. PLANTAGINACEÆ.

233. PLANTAGO L.   Plantain, Ribwort.

> 377. P. LANCEOLATA. Roadsides, yards, etc., becoming abundant. Introduced. Ashland (Williams); Lincoln (Webber, Smith, Williams); Crete (Swezey); Aurora (Bessey).

> 378. P. PATAGONICA Jacq. var. ARISTATA (Michx.) Gray. Hastings (Bessey).

96. OLEACEÆ.

234. FRAXINUS L.   Ash.

> 379. F. AMERICANA L. White ash. Sarpy and Nemaha Counties (Bessey).

97. GENTIANACEÆ.

235. GENTIANA L.   Gentian.

> 380. G. FLAVIDA Gray. (*G. alba.* Muhl.) White Gentian. Low ground. Nemaha Co., Aug. (Webber); Weeping Water (Williams).

236. MENYANTHES L.   Buckbean.

> 381. M. TRIFOLIATA L. Ponds, Cherry County (Bessey).

237. ERYTHRÆA Richard.   Centaury.

> 382. E. DOUGLASII Gray. On the sands of the Platte River in Scott's Bluff Co., Aug. 1 (Rydberg).

98. ASCLEPIADACEÆ.

238. ACERATES Ell.   Green milkweed.

383. A. AURICULATA Engelm. Lewellen, rare (Swezey). "Sand-draws" in Deuel Co., July (Rydberg).

It is easily mistaken for *Asclepias stenophylla* from which it can not be distinguished except by the form of the hood and its auricles (Rydberg).

384. A. VIRIDIFLORA (Raf.) Ell. var. LANCEOLATA (Ives) Gray. Hills, Wahoo, June, 1890 (Rydberg).

99. COMPOSITÆ.

239. STEPHANOMERIA Nutt.

385. S. MINOR Nutt. "Bad lands" north of Scott's Bluff, July 22. It is easily mistaken for a *Lygodesmia* (Rydberg).

240. LACTUCA L.   Lettuce.

386. L. INTEGRIFOLIA Bigel. Roadsides, Weeping Water (Williams).

241. CREPIS L.

387. C. INTERMEDIA Gray. Side of cañon, plentiful. War Bonnet, June (Williams).

388. C. RUNCINATA (James) Torr. & Gr. Collected by Rev. Bates at Valentine (Rydberg). Lewellen (Swezey). Platte bottoms, Cheyenne Co., July 3; Pumpkin Seed Valley, July 14 (Rydberg).

242. CICHORIUM L.   Succory, Chicory.

389. C. INTYBUS L. Yards, Lincoln, Introduced (Webber).

243. CNICUS L.   Thistle.

390. C. ALTISSIMUS (L.) Willd. var. FILIPENDULUS Gray. Belmont (Swezey).

391. C. UNDULATUS (Nutt.) Gray, var. CANESCENS (Nutt.) Gray. Prairies, common. Antelope Co., Pine Ridge, July–Aug.

A form from Pine Ridge has conspicuously decurrent leaves, a character shown also by a specimen of Hayden's in the Engelmann Herbarium from the Sand hills of the Plains.

Cnicus pitcheri Torr., No. 1738 of the Cat. of the Fl. of Nebr. belongs here (Webber).

392. C. UNDULATUS (Nutt.) Gray, var. MEGACEPHALUS Gray. Broken Bow, July 4 (Webber).

244. ARNICA L.

393. A. CORDIFOLIA Hook. Hillsides, rare. Squaw Cañon, Pine Ridge, July (Williams).

245. HELENIUM L.

394. H. AUTUMNALE L. Sneeze-weed. Collected by Rev. Bates at Valentine (Rydberg); Minden (Hapeman).

246. PECTIS L.

395. P. ANGUSTIFOLIA Torr. " Sand draws " Deuel Co., July.

A little plant (1-3 in. high) with glandular punctate leaves and pleasant odor (Rydberg).

247. THELESPERMA Lees.

396. T. AMBIGUUM Gray. Prairies, quite common. Long Pine (Swezey); Alliance, July; Crawford, Aug.; Belmont, July (Webber).

397. T. FILIFOLIUM (Hook.) Gray. Table land, Banner Co., Aug. Collected also by Rev. Bates at Valentine (Rydberg).

248. COREOPSIS L.   Tickseed.

398. C. ARISTOSA Michx. Long Pine (Swezey).

399. C. TRICHOSPERMA (?) Michx. var. TENUILOBA Gray. Lewellen, Alliance (Swezey in Nebr. Flowering Plants). (This has the character of *Thelesperma* and will likely prove to be near *T. ambiguum*. — Webber).

249. HELIANTHUS L.   Sunflower.

400. H. DECAPETALUS (?) L. Crete (Swezey Nebr. Flowering Plants, p. 10).

(This is near *H. tuberosus* L. to which it may have to be referred.— Webber).

250. ECLIPTA L.

401. E. ALBA (L.) Haussk. Crete (Swezey).

251. FRANSERIA Cav.

402. F. HOOKERIANA Nutt. Alliance (Swezey). Lodge Pole Creek, near Potter, Aug. 15 (Rydberg).

403. F. TOMENTOSA Gray. Becoming a troublesome weed on low rich soil in Kearney Co. (Rydberg).

252. AMBROSIA L.   Ragweed.

404. A. TRIFIDA L. var. INTEGRIFOLIA (Muhl.) Torr & Gr. With the type in various places. At Hackberry Springs only this form was found (Rydberg); Lincoln (Bessey); Minden (Hapeman).

253. IVA L.

405. I. AXILLARIS Pursh. Near Platte River, Scott's Bluff Co., July 25 (Rydberg).

254. ANTENNARIA Gærtn.   Everlasting.

406. A. DIMORPHA Torr. & Gr. Collected at Harrison by Rev. Bates (Bessey).

407. A. DIOICA (L.) Gaertn. Alliance (Swezey); Belmont, July 14 (Webber).

255. ERIGERON L.   Fleabane.

408. E. CANUS Gray. Lawrence Fork, Banner Co., Aug. (Rydberg).

409. E. CÆSPITOSUS Nutt. Prairies, not uncommon. Hat Creek Basin, Aug.: Belmont, July (Webber).

410. E. CONCINNUS Torr. & Gray. Dry prairies. War Bonnet, June (Williams).

411. E. MACRANTHUS Nutt. Cañons, etc. Hat Creek Basin, Aug. 2. (Prof. Swezey's specimens of *E. glabellus* Nutt. from Long Pine (Neb. Flowering Plants, p. 9) probably belong here, although differing somewhat from the type in having a hairy involucre. My specimens also show this peculiarity but were pronounced by Dr. Watson to be *E. macranthus.*— Webber.)

412. E. PUMILUS Nutt. Collected by Rev. Bates at Valentine (Rydberg); War Bonnet, June (Williams); Lewellen (Swezey); Pine Ridge, July; Hat Creek Basin, Aug. (Webber).

Quite common on dry prairies.

256. ASTER L. Aster.

413. A. AZUREUS Lindl. Weeping Water (Williams).

414. A. ERICÆFOLIUS Rothrock. Prairies, Venango, Perkins Co., June 23 (Rydberg).

415. A. FOLIACEUS Lindl. Platte River north of Scott's Bluff, July 23; Horse Creek, Aug. 1; Lodge Pole Creek, near Kimball, Aug. 12 (Rydberg).

416. A. PANICULATUS Lam. Low prairies, very common, Lincoln, Sept. (Webber).

417. A. PUNICEUS L. Prairies. Clear water, Antelope Co., Sept. (Webber).

418. A. TRADESCANTI L. Crete, common (Swezey, Nebr. Fl. Pl , p. 9.) (The specimens of this seem to me to be nearer *A. paniculatus.* Its occurrence in Nebraska needs confirmation. — Webber.)

257. TOWNSENDIA Hook.

419. T. SERICEA Hook. Prairies, not uncommon. Collected by Dr. W. A. Thomas in Hayes Co., April (Rydberg); McCook; Alliance; Ogalalla (Swezey); Antelope Co. (Webber).

258. SOLIDAGO L. Golden rod.

420. S. CANADENSIS L. var. PROCERA Torr. & Gr. Weeping Water (Williams).

421. S. NEMORALIS Ait. var. INCANA (Torr. & Gr.) Gray. Hills, Deuel Co., Aug. (Rydberg); Lewellen: Alliance; Lodge Pole Creek; Belmont (Swezey).

422. S. RADULA Nutt. Edges of thickets, Weeping Water (Williams).

423. S. SEROTINA Ait. var. GIGANTEA (Ait.) Gray. Saunders Co., Sept. (Rydberg).

424. S. SPECIOSA Nutt. Prairies, Ashland, June (Williams).

259. HAPLOPAPPUS Cass.

425. H. NUTTALLII Torr. & Gr. "Sand draws," of Banner Co. (Rydberg). Denuded places, in " Bad Lands," Hat Creek Basin, Sioux Co., Aug. (Webber).

426. H. RUBIGINOSUS (?) Torr. & Gr.   Lodge Pole Creek (Swezey, Nebr. Fl. Pl., p. 9).

(Prof. Swezey's specimens are rather meager to decide upon, and as Nebraska is somewhat out of the known range of the species, its occurrence may perhaps remain in question until confirmed.)

260. CHRYSOPSIS Nutt.   Golden aster.

427. C. VILLOSA (Pursh) Nutt. var. CANESCENS (DC.) Gray. " Sand draws," Deuel and Banner Co.'s (Rydberg).

428. C. VILLOSA (Pursh) Nutt. var. HISPIDA (Hook.) Gray. " Sand draws," Deuel Co. (Rydberg). Long Pine (Conklin, Swezey).

429. C. VILLOSA (Pursh) Nutt. var. SESSILIFLORA (Nutt.) Gray. " Sand draws," Banner Co. (Rydberg).

261. BRICKELLIA Ell.

430. B. GRANDIFLORA (Hook.) Nutt.   In a cañon, Banner Co. (Rydberg).

262. VERNONIA Schreb.   Iron weed.

431. V. ALTISSIMA Nutt. Banks, etc.   Wahoo, Saunders Co., Sept. (Rydberg).

432. V. NOVEBORACENSIS (L.) Willd.   Bottom meadows, Ashland, Aug. (Williams).

SUPPLEMENTARY LIST OF RECENTLY REPORTED SPECIES.

BY CHARLES E. BESSEY, PH.D.

Species determined by Rev. J. M. Bates of Valentine, are marked (B.); those by A. T. Bell and W. H. Skinner of the Crete High school, (B. & S.); those by F. C. Clements, a student in my laboratory, (C.); those by Dr. H. Hapeman of Minden, (H.); tnose by Roscoe Pound, formerly assistant in my laboratory, (P.); those by P. A. Rydberg, a graduate student, (R.); those by J. R. Schofield, a student in my laboratory, (S.); those by Professor G D. Swezey of Doane College, (Sw.); those by A. F. Woods, assistant in my laboratory, (W).

MYXOMYCETES.

1. *Perithœna flavida* Peck. On rotten logs. Crete, Nov. 1891, (B. & S.)
2. *Trichia chrysosperma* (Bull) DC. On rotten logs. Crete, Nov 1891, (B. & S.)
3. *Trichia varia* Pers. Crete, Nov. 1891, (B. & S)
4. *Arcyria punicea* Pers. Crete, Nov. 1891, (B. & S.)
5. *Arcyria adnata* (Batsch.) Rost. Crete, Nov. 1891, (B. & S)
6. *Arcyria nutans* (Bull) Grev. Crete, Nov. 1891, (B. & S.)
7. *Hemiarcyria serpula* Scop On bark, Lincoln, (C.)
8. *Comatricha friesiana* (D. By.) Rost. On rotten wood in a dark well York, Apr. 1892, (Bessey.)
9. *Stemonitis ferruginea* Ehrb. Crete, Nov. 1891, (B. & S.)
10. *Chondrioderma radiatum* (Linn.) Rost. Crete, Nov. 1891, (B. & S)

BACTERIACEÆ.

11. *Bacterium aceti* (Kuetz.) Lanzi. In fermenting cider. Lincoln, Feb 1892, (Bessey.)
12. *Beggiatoa pellucida* Cohn. Lincoln, (W.)

NOSTOCACEÆ.

13. *Microcoleus terrestsis* Desm. var. *repens* Kuetz. In greenhouse. Lincoln, Feb. 1892, (Bessey.)
14. *Nostoc muscorum* Ag. On moss leaf from Valentine, (C.)
15. *Oscillaria froelichii* Kuetz. var. *fusca* Kirch. In greenhouse. Lincoln, Feb. 1892, (Bessey)
16. *Oscillaria gracillima* Kuetz. In the basin of the artesian well, Lincoln, Dec. 1891, (S.)

17. *Oscillaria princeps* Vauch. Lincoln, July, 1891, (W.)
18. *Lyngbya æstuarii* Liebm. Forming a reddish-brown coating upon the ground near Lincoln, the soil probably somewhat saline. April, 1892, (Bessey.)
19. *Isactis fluviatilis* (Rab.) Kirch. Minden, (H.)

PALMELLACEÆ.
20. *Protococcus frustulosus* (Carm.) D. Ton. In the basin of the artesian well, Lincoln, Dec. 1891, (S)
21. *Protococcus vestitus* Reinsch. In material collected by Dr. Hapeman at Minden, (C.)
22. *Raphidium braunii* Naeg. In material from Minden collected by Dr. Hapeman, (C.)
22½. *Raphidum polymorphum* Fries. var. *aciculare* A. Br. Minden, (H.)
23. *Tetraspora lubrica* (Roth.) Ag. Minden, Coll. Hapeman, (W.)

CLADOPHORACEÆ.
24. *Cladophora glomerata* (L.) Kuetz., var. *simplicior* Kuetz. Minden, Coll. by Dr. Hapeman. (W.)
25. *Draparnaldia plumosa* Ag. Wahoo, (R.)
26. *Draparnaldia glomerata* (Vauch.) Ag. var. *genuina* Kirch.   In a pool. Lincoln, (W.)
27. *Chaetophora cornu-damæ* (Roth.) Ag. var. *polyclados* Kuetz.   Minden, Coll. Hapeman, (W.)

DESMIDIACEÆ.
28. *Desmidium aptogonium* Breb. Minden, Coll. Hapeman, (C.)
29. *Closterium acerosum* (Schr.) Ehrb. Lincoln, (C.)
30. *Closterium dianæ* Ehrb. Lincoln, (C.)
31. *Closterium intermedium* Ralfs. Minden, Coll. Hapeman, (C.)
32. *Closterium lanceolatum* Kuetz. Lincoln, (W.)
33. *Cosmarium gotlandicum* Wittr. Minden, Coll. Hapeman, (C.)
34. *Cosmarium botrytis* Menegh. In material collected by Dr. Hapeman at Minden, (C.)
35. *Cosmarium portianum* Arch. Minden, Coll. Hapeman, (C.)
36. *Euastrum pokornyanum* Grun. In material collected at Minden by Dr. Hapeman, (C.)
37. *Staurastrum dickiei* Ralfs. In material collected at Minden by Dr. Hapeman, (C.)
38. *Staurastrum eustephanum* (Ehr?) Ralfs. In material collected at Minden by Dr. Hapeman, (C.)
39. *Staurastrum quadrangulare* Breb. In material collected at Minden by Dr. Hapeman, (C.)

DIATOMACEÆ.
40. *Stauroneis lineata* Kg. Agrees with Wolle's figure, but no description is accessible. In material from Minden, collected by Dr. Hapeman, (C.)
41. *Stauroneis phœnicenteron* (Nitzsch.) Ehr. Lincoln, (C.)
42. *Navicula formosa* Greg. Lincoln, (C.)
43. *Navicula hemiptera* Kg. Crete, (C.)
44. *Navicula mutica* Kg. Lincoln, (C.)

45 *Navicula rhomboides* Ehrb.   In material collected at Minden by Dr. Hapeman, (C.)

46 *Pleurosigma spenceri* (Quek.) W. Sm.   Lincoln, (C.)

47 *Gomphonema dichotomum* Kuetz.   Minden, (H.)

48 *Gomphonema geminatum* S. & F.   Minden, (H.)

49 *Cocconeis striata* Ehrb.   In material collected at Minden by Dr. Hapeman, (C.)

50. *Epithemia argus* Kuetz.   Minden, (H.)   This species was doubtfully recorded in the catalogue (No. 100) as from Lincoln.

51. *Epithemia sorex* Kuetz.   Pauline, (H.)

52. *Epithemia zebra* (Ehr.) Kuetz.   Minden, (H.)

53. *Synedra affinis* Kuetz.   Minden, in material coll. by Dr. Hapeman, (C.)

54 *Synedra ulna* (Nitzsch) Ehr. var. *longissima* (W. Sm.) Brun.   In material collected at Minden by Dr. Hapeman, (C).

55. *Fragilaria virescens* Ralfs.   Minden, in material collected by Dr. Hapeman, (C.)

56. *Nitzschia communis* Rabb.   In the basin of the artesian well. Lincoln, Dec. 1891, (S.)

57 *Nitzschia thermalis* (Ehr.) Auersw.   In salt water.   Lincoln, (C.)

58. *Nitzschia vermicularis* (Kg.) Hantz.   Minden, (H.)

59. *Nitzschia vitrea* Norm.   Minden, (H.)

60. *Nitzschia vivax* W. Sm.   Minden, (H.)

ZYGNEMACE.E

61. *Mougeotia genuflexa* (Dillw.) Ag.   Lincoln, (C.)

62. *Zygnema pectinatum* (Vauch.) Ag., var. *anomalum* (Hass.) Kirch.   Minden, Coll. by Dr. Hapeman, (W.)

63. *Spirogyra crassa* Kuetz.   South Bend, (C.)   Filaments 136 mmm. in diameter.

OEDOGONIACE.E.

64. *Oedogonium pringsheimii* Cram   Minden, Coll. Hapeman, (W.)

65. *Oedogonium wolleanum* Wittr.   Minden, Coll. Hapeman, (C.)

COLEOCHETACE.E.

66. *Coleochaete scutata* Breb.   In material from Minden, collected by Dr. Hapeman, (C.)

SPILERIACE.E.

67. *Xylaria polymorpha* (Pers.) Grev., var. *spathulata* Pers.   Lincoln, (C.)

68 *Xylaria polymorpha* (Pers.) Grev., var. *acrodactyla* Nits.   Lincoln, (C.)

69. *Hypoxylon epiphloeum* B. & C.   Lincoln, (W.)

DOTHIDIACE.E.

70 *Dothidia ribesia* Pers.   Lincoln. On stems of *Ribes gracile* Michx. (W.)

PEZIZACE.E.

71. *Lachnea scutellata* Linn.   On earth in greenhouse.   Lincoln, (C.)

72 *Sclerotinia dureaeana* Tul.   On ground in woods.   Lincoln, Apr. 1892, (C.)

73 *Sclerotinia trifoliorum* Eriks.   Raymond, (C.)

74. *Sclerotinia gracilis* Clements, n. sp.   Cup thin, hemispherical, bright brown, margin entire, darker: stipe elongated, flexuous, thick, 1.5—

2 cm. long: asci cylindrical, attenuated at base, 150—160 x 10 mmm. ascospores 8, oblong-elliptical, curved, biguttulate, 26—32 x 10—11: mmm.: paraphyses filiform slightly clavate at apex, somewhat branched. Sclerotium black, thin, coriaceous, forked, ⅓ x 1½ cm. In shady woods, near Lincoln, Nebr., (associated with *Erythronium albidum.'*)   The cups are from 2½ to 3½ mm. broad, a single stipe arising from each of the two to three forks of the sclerotium.

75.   *Phialea aquatica* (Curr.) Sacc.   Muddy banks.   Raymond. (C.)
76.   *Belonidium aurelia* (Pers.) De Not.   Lincoln, on stumps, (C.)

HELVELLACE.E.

77.   *Verpa digitaliformis* Pers.   In woods under trees.   Raymond, May 1892, (C.)

UREDINE.E.

78.   *Puccinia buchloes* Schofield, n. sp.   III.   Amphigenous, or mostly hy-pophyllus: sori scattered, or more or less linear-clustered, epidermis of host plant splitting and supporting the edges of the sori: spores broadly elliptical, or slightly obovate, 13 to 23 broad by 29 to 36 m mm. long, mostly about 22 by 31 mmm., epispore smooth, light-brown, constricted at the septum, slightly thickened at the apex, which is obtusely rounded: pedicel stout, once or twice the length of the spore, tinted.   On *Buchloe dactyloides* Engelm.   Collected by J. G. Smith, Lincoln, Nebr., Oct. 1886.

USTILAGINE.E.

79.   *Sorosporium cuneatum* Schofield, n. sp.   Glomerules nearly globose, 38 to 48 mmm. in diameter, mostly about 44.5 mmm., bright brown, composed of from forty to fifty spores: spores 9 5 to 11 mmm. long, crowded, and in optical section cuneate in outline, all minutely roughened on the basal (exposed) surface.

In flower heads and stems of *Grindelia squarrosa* Dunal.   Lincoln, Nebr., in the autumn of 1891.

The fungus attacks not only the heads, completely destroying the achenes, but it attacks the stem also, producing gall-like enlarge-ments.   The spores in the stem are formed immediately under the bark.

In California, according to Dr. Harkness, *Sorosporium californicum* Hark. attacks *Grindelia robusta* Nutt., reducing the flower-heads to one-third their natural size.   In Nebraska the same reduction oc-curs on the lower branches of *Grindelia squarrosa* Dunal., but on the upper branches the parasite has the opposite effect, enlarging the heads to more than double their natural size.

MUCEDINE.E.

80.   *Verticillium rufum* (Schwabe.) Rebh.   On sugar beets in silo.   Lin-coln, (P.)

LYCOPERDACE.E.

81.   *Lycoperdon cepaeforme* Bull.   Lincoln, (C.)
82.   *Lycoperdon peckii* Morg.   Lincoln, (C.)

AGARICINE.E

83. *Hiatula crenulata* Fr. Prairies, Lincoln, (C.)

84. *Hebeloma crustuliniforme* Bull. Lincoln, (C.)

85. *Coprinus comatus* Fl. D. Lincoln, (W.)

86. *Coprinus plicatilis* (Curt) Fr. Lincoln, (Bessey)

POLYPORE.E.

87. *Polystictus pergamenus* Fr. Lincoln, (W.)

THELEPHORE.E.

88. *Stereum versicolor* (Schw) Fr., var *fasciata* Schw. Lincoln, (W.)

CHARACE.E.

89. *Chara foetida* A. Br. Collected by J. M. Bates at Valentine, (Bessey)

EQUISETACE.E.

90. *Equisetum limosum* L. Platte river bottom, Kearney Co., June 15, 1891. (R.)

91. *Equisetum pratensis* Ehrh. Sowbelly Canon, Sioux Co , Aug 1890, (Bessey.)

92. *Equisetum hyemale* L. Collected by J. M. Bates at Ft. Niobrara, (Bessey.)

CYPERACE.E.

93. *Carex marcida* Boott. var. *debilis* Bailey, Deuel Co., (R.)

94. *Heleocharis compressa* Sull. Ewing. (B.)

GRAMINE.E.

95. *Elymus sibiricus* L. Sioux Co. (B.)

96. *Elymus striatus* Willd., var. *villosus* Gr. Long Pine, (B.)

97. *Agropyrum violaceum* Lange. North-western Nebraska. (B.)

98. *Festuca confinis* Vasey., var. ———— Harrison and Crawford, July 1891, (B.)

99 *Poa alpina* L. McColligan canon, Deuel Co., June 26, 1891, (R.)

100. *Glyceria distans* Wahl., var. *airoides* (L.) Wahl. Lodge Pole creek, near Sidney, Aug. 19, 1891, (R.)

101. *Koeleria cristata* Pers., var. *gracilis* Gray. Prairie, Deuel Co., June 25, 1891, (R.)

102. *Arrhenatherum avenaceum* Beauv. Lincoln, June 12, 1891, (R.)

103. *Calamagrostis confinis* Nutt. Platte River, Kearney, Co., June 15, 1891, (R)

104. *Sporobolus cryptandrus* (Trin.) Gr., var. (near) *flexuosus* Thurb. The pedicels are capillary, but not drooping. Dry sandy soil near Scott's Bluff, July 24, 1891, (R.)

105. *Sporobolus confusus* Towen. This is the *S. serotinus* of the "Contributions from the Botanical Department of the University of Nebraska. New Series, II.," page 6. Sands of Platte, near Horse creek, Scott's Bluff Co., Aug 1, 1891, (R.)

106. *Sporobolus minor* Vasey. Long Pine, (B.)

107 *Muhlenbergia racemosa* (Michx.) B. S. P., var. *ramosa* Vasey. Common westward, (B.)

108 *Aristida oligantha* Michx. Cherry Co., (B.)

109. *Panicum crus-galli* L. var. *muticum* Vasey. This is without any doubt indigenous. Canon in Kiwa Valley, Scott's Bluff Co., July 28, 1891, (R.)

110. *Panicum dichotomum* L. var. *barbulatum* (Michx.) Gray. Platte river bottom, Kearney Co., June 15. 1891, (R.)

111. *Panicum virgatum* L., var. *confertum* Vasey. Banner Co., (R.)

JUNCACE.E.

112. *Juncus balticus* Deth. North Platte river, Cheyenne Co., July 3, 1891, (R.)

113. *Juncus marginatus* Rost. Minden, (H.)

114. *Juncus tenuis* Willd., var. *congestus* Engelm. Kennedy, (B.)

LILIACE.E.

115. *Trillium nivale* Riddell. Weeping Water, Apr. 1892, (Miss Rands.)

116. *Zygadenus nuttallii* Gray. In fruit, Hills of Pumpkin Seed Valley, July 6, 1891, (R.)

IRIDACE.E.

117. *Sisyrinchium anceps* Cav. Spring south of Pumpkin Seed Valley, July 14, 1891, (R.)

POLYGONACE.E.

118. *Polygonum aviculare* L. var. *parva* Holz. var. nov. Stem much branched, low, prostrate, branchlets with very short joints, nearly covered by the sheaths, which are strongly ribbed and brown at the base; the scarious tips long, loose, aristate; leaves crowded, oblong 2-3 lines long; flowers minute, reddish or brownish. According to Mr. J. M. Holzinger, it has been collected by Wright in 1851 in N. Mex., and by Newberry (?) near Dallas, Texas. Spring, Deuel Co., Aug. 24, 1891, (R.)

NYCTAGINACE.E.

119. *Abronia micrantha* Dougl. Court House Rock, Cheyenne, Co., July 4, 1891, (R.)

CARYOPHYLLACE.E.

120. *Arenaria franklinii* Dougl. Court House Rock, Cheyenne Co., July 4, and cliffs in Banner and Scott's Bluff Cos., July–Aug. 1891, (R.)

RANUNCULACE.E.

121. *Clematis douglasii* Hook., var. *scottii* Porter. Reported by Professor Swezey from Sheridan Co.

CRUCIFER.E.

122. *Stanleya pinnatifida* Nutt. Reported by Professor Swezey from Sheridan Co.

123. *Draba nemorosa* Ledb. Alliance, (Bessey.)

124. *Nasturtium curvisiliqua* Nutt. Near a well 1½ miles from the Wyoming line, Scott's Bluffs Co., July 31, 1891, (R.)

CISTACE.E.

125. *Lechea minor* L. Minden, collected by Dr. Hapeman, (W.)

HYPERICACE.E.

126. *Hypericum ascyron* L. Cass Co., (Sw.)

POLYGALACE.E.

127 *Polygala sanguinea* L.   Atkinson and Neligh, (B.)

UMBELLIFER.E.

128. *Cicuta bulbifera* L.   Cherry Co.   Not in fruit, (B.)

129. *Osmorhiza claytoni* (Michx.) B. S. P.   Cass Co., (Sw.)

130. *Musenium divaricatum* Nutt.   Harrison, (B.)

131 *Peucedanum kingii* Watson.   This, possibly, should be included in the genus Pseudocymopterus Coult. and Rose, as the dorsal ribs are more or less winged.   Scott's Pass, July 22, 1891, (R.)

SAXIFRAGACE.E.

132. *Ribes setosum* Lindl.   Dawes Co., (Sw.)

LOASACE.E

133. *Mentzelia albicaulis* (Hook.) Dougl.   Scott's Bluffs Co., (R.)   In the specimens collected the seeds are muricate, but the leaves are nearly entire or more rarely sinuately toothed.

HALORAGE.E.

134. *Callitriche verna* L.   Kennedy, July 1891, (B.)

ROSACE.E.

135. *Cratægus subvillosa* Schrad.   Sarpy and Cass counties, (Sw.)

136. *Rosa nutkana* Presl.   Curtis, Frontier Co., June 22.   McColligan canon, Deuel Co., June 26, 1891, (R.)

LEGUMINOS.E.

137. *Desmodium illinoense* Gray.   Reported from Cass Co., by Professor Swezey.

138. *Oxytropis multiceps* Nutt.   Hills of upper Lawrence Fork, Kimball Co., Aug. 10; in fruit, (R.)

139. *Astragalus bisulcatus* Gray.   Dakota Junction, May, 1891, (B.)

140. (?) *Astragalus pubentissimus* Torr. and Gray.   Canon in Gosper Co., June 20; Hills near Curtis, Frontier Co., June 22; Lawrence Fork, Banner Co., July 8; near Kimball, Aug. 12, 1891, (R.)

141 *Amorpha microphylla* Pursh.   Fragments covered with rust seen in the possession of Mr. Schofield, and said to have been collected near Lincoln, Sept. 1891, (R.)

POLEMONIACE.E.

142. *Gilia sp*————.   Glandular pubescent; root biennial, possibly perennial, stem branched above, 1 foot high or higher; leaves somewhat irregularly pinnatifid; lobes linear, not wider than the rachis, somewhat fleshy, mucronate; flowers in a branched panicle; corolla violet or blue with a whitish tube, somewhat funnel-form 2 lines long; stamens exserted; calyx with prominent ribs.   The plant is more or less glandular all over.   Mr. John Holzinger of the Department of Agriculture has named it Gilia pinnatifida, which without any doubt, it is not, as the plant is more branched, more glandular, the division of the leaves few and longer and narrower, and the corolla smaller and not at all salverform.   It stands nearer G. inconspicua, from which (if distinct) it differs in being more robust,

more branched, and, perhaps, more glandular. Sands of North Platte near Horse Creek, Aug. 1, 1891, (R.)

143. *Gilia spicata* Nutt. Banner Co., (R.)

144. *Phlox bryoides* Nutt. Hills of upper Lawrence Fork, Aug. 11, 1891, (R.)

BORRAGINACE.E.

145. (?) *Oreocarya sericea* (Gray) Greene. (Pittonia I. p. 58.) In fruit only. McColligan Canon, Deuel Co., June 26; upper Lawrence Fork, Kimball Co., Aug. 10, 1891, (R.)

By an oversight an error was made on page 37, under *Cryptanthe*, *Krynitzkia glomerata* Gray. is changed to *C. glomerata* Lehmann. It should have been given as *Oreocarya glomerata* (Pursh) Greene. (Pittonia, I. p. 58.) (R.)

146. *Allocarya californica* (Fisch. and Meyer.) Greene. *Krynitzkia californica* (Fisch. and Meyer.) Gray Reported from Dawes County by Professor Swezey.

SOLANACE.E.

147, *Physalis mollis* Nutt. var. *cinerascens* Gray. The leaves are broadly ovate, 2 in. long, angulately toothed or repand, very thin; pubescence stellate or simple (even a little glandular,) very short, except on the calyx, the pedicels, the petioles and younger parts of the stem, where it is long and soft; petioles as long as the leaves or longer; corolla greenish-yellow with a darker spot; anthers yellow; fruiting calyx globose-ovate. Under the cliffs on the south side of Scott's Bluff, July 20, 1891, (R.)

148. *Physalis sp.* (near *P. hederæfolia* Gray.) Leaves scarcely over 1 in. long, ovate, thickish; petioles generally shorter than the blades; fruiting calyx globose, about 1 in.; pubescence short, with a few long hairs, a little glandular. According to Mr. Holzinger it stands nearest P. hederæfolia, but it differs from the description of that species in Gray's Synoptical Flora, in that the pedicels are much longer, the leaves, larger and less toothed, and that it is very little glandular. It approaches P. fendleri. Prairies near Ashford, Banner Co., Aug. 6, (R.)

149. (?) *Physalis palmeri* Gray Leaves thickish, ovate, angulately toothed; petioles of the length of the blade which is 1-1½ in.; fruiting calyx ovate, (about an inch) on a slender pedicel. Stem low and nearly prostrate, strong scented; pubescence viscid, with short hairs. Sandy banks of a draw southwest of Sidney, Aug. 18. P. palmeri has been collected in southeast California, and this is entirely out of its supposed range. It may, therefore, be something else, (R.)

150. *Physalis longifolia* Nutt. (*P. lanceolata* Michx. var. *lævigata* Gray.) I believe that this has a very good right to be separated from P. lanceolata. as the berry is *yellow*, stalked in the calyx which is ovate, less angled and *not sunken* at the base; the bottom of the calyx, stipe, and lower part of the berry *glutinous*, as if it were *painted* with *molasses*. Lawrence Fork, Banner Co., July 8; Kimball, Aug. 12, 1891, (R.)

151. *Physalis viscosa* L. var. *spathulæfolia* Gray. Low, 6-10 in. high, prostrate or nearly upright; pubescence short and stiff, or more

commonly, scarcely any except on the calyx, where it is hispid, leaves obovate or spatulate, tapering into the petiole, nearly entire; fruiting calyx globose-ovate, scarcely angled, very little sunken at the base; berry yellowish green, corolla ½ in. wide, greenish-yellow with a darker spot. In P. lanceolata it is ²₃ ¾ in. wide and ochroleucous. Sand draws of Western Nebraska, June and Aug. This is the same as P. lanceolata, No. 2 on page 38 preceding, (R.)

SCROPHULARIACEÆ.

152. *Seymeria macrophylla* Nutt. Reported by Professor Swezey from Cass Co.

153. *Gratiola virginiana* L. Kennedy, July 1891. (B.)

154. *Pentstemon acuminatus* Dougl. Deuel Co. (R).

155. *Linaria canadensis* Dumont. Ewing, June 1891. Collected by Mr. Bates. (Bessey.)

ASCLEPIADACEÆ.

156. *Asclepias stenophylla* (Gray). In the April (1892) number of the *Botanical Gazette* J. M. Holzinger of the National Herbarium shows that what have been taken to be two distinct species viz: *Asclepias stenophylla* Gray. (No. 1677 of the catalogue), and *Acerates auriculata* Engelm. (No. 383 of the Appendix) are in reality but one species of Asclepias. In a subsequent note (*Bot. Gaz.* May) Mr. Holzinger shows that Gray's name must be retained.

CAPRIFOLIACEÆ.

157. *Lonicera hirsuta* Eaton. Ft. Niobrara, Aug. 1891. (B.)

COMPOSITÆ.

158. *Cnicus pitcheri* Torr. The true C. pitcheri is common in the sand hill regions of Kearney Co., July 15; rare in Banner Co., July 6, (R.)

159. *Cnicus virginiana* Pursh. Minden. Anther tips bluntish instead of "subulate." Collected by Dr. Hapeman, (W.)

160. *Crepis tectorum* L. In a lawn in Chadron, 1891, (B.)

161. *Gaillardia pulchella* Fong. Franklin Co., Sept. 1891, (R.)

162. *Actinella scaposa* Nutt. var. *linearis* Nutt. Franklin Co., (Sw.)

163. (?) *Chaenactis douglasii* Hook and Arn., var. *alpina* Gray. The material was too incomplete for identification. A low cespitose, tomentose plant with pinnately parted leaves, and scapiform stem 3 6 in. high, with a few heads. Upper Lawrence Fork, Kimball County Aug. 10, (R)

164. (?) *Aster adscendens* Lindl. Lodge Pole Creek, Kimball, Aug. 12, 1891. (R.)

165. (?) *Aster fremontii* Gray. Horse Creek, Scott's Bluff Co., Aug. 1 1891, (R.)

166. *Aster tradescantii* L. Big Springs, Deuel Co., Aug. 24, 1891, (R.) (See No. 418 of Mr. Webber's "Appendix.")

167. *Bigelovia graveolens* Gr. var. *glabrata* Gray. Canon of Scott's Bluff Co., Aug. 6, (R.)

168. *Bigelovia howardii* Gray. Hills of Banner and Scott's Bluff counties. July-Aug. 1891, (R.)

169. *Haplopappus armerioides* Gray. Hills in Banner Co.; July 6, 1891, (R.)

170. *Liatris spicata* Willd. Platte River bottom, Scott's Bluff Co., Aug. 3, 1891, (R)

GENERIC INDEX.

www.ingramcontent.com/pod-product-compliance
Lightning Source LLC
Chambersburg PA
CBHW021640270326
41931CB00008B/1103